W9-DCE-462

Apple Pro Training Series

Logic Pro X 10.4

David Nahmani

Apple
Certified

Apple Pro Training Series
Logic Pro X 10.4
David Nahmani
Copyright © 2018 by David Nahmani
Updated for Logic Pro X v10.4 May 2018

Peachpit Press
www.peachpit.com
Peachpit Press is an imprint of Pearson Education, Inc.
To report errors, please send a note to errata@peachpit.com.

Apple Series Editor: Laura Norman
Editor: Bob Lindstrom
Senior Production Editor: Tracey Croom
Production Coordinator: Maureen Forys, Happenstance Type-O-Rama
Technical Editor: John Moores
Copy Editor: Bob Lindstrom
Proofreader: Scout Festa
Compositor: Cody Gates, Happenstance Type-O-Rama
Indexer: Valerie Perry
Cover Illustration: Paul Mavrides
Cover Production: Cody Gates, Happenstance Type-O-Rama

ISBN 13: 978-0-13-524476-0
ISBN 10: 0-13-5244765
1 18

Acknowledgments I would like to express my thanks to my wife, Nathalie, and to my sons, Liam and Dylan, for their support and encouragement; to my editors Bob Lindstrom, John Moores, and Laura Norman for being by my side and enabling me to write the best book I could write.

My deepest gratitude to the artists and producers who agreed to provide their Logic sessions for this book: Distant Cousins for their songs "Raise It Up" and "BIG," Televisor for their song "Alliance," and Matt McJunkins from the Beta Machine for helping me write and produce the song "Little Lady."

Contents at a Glance

Table of Contents

Getting Started

Welcome to the official Apple Pro Training Series course for
Logic Pro X 10.4. This book is a comprehensive introduction to professional music production with Logic Pro X 10.4. It uses real-world music and hands-on exercises to teach you how to record, edit, arrange, mix, produce, and polish audio and MIDI files in a professional workflow.
So let's get started!

The Methodology

This book takes a hands-on approach to learning the software, so you'll be working through the project files and media you download from www.peachpit.com. It's divided into lessons that introduce the interface elements and ways of working with them, building progressively until you can comfortably grasp the entire application and its standard workflows.

Each lesson in this book is designed to support the concepts learned in the preceding lesson, and first-time readers should go through the book from start to finish. However, each lesson is self-contained, so when you need to review a topic, you can quickly jump to any lesson.

The book is designed to guide you through the music production process as it teaches Logic. The lessons are organized into four sections.

Lessons 1–3: Exploring the Interface and Working with Real Instruments

In this section, you'll explore the fundamentals of Logic Pro X, and learn to record and edit audio.

Lesson 1 starts you out with an overview of the entire process. You'll become familiar with the interface and the various ways to navigate a project; use Apple loops to build a song from scratch; and then arrange, mix, and export the song to an MP3 file.

Lessons 2 and 3 dive deeper into typical situations you may encounter when recording from microphones or other audio sources. You'll edit recordings to select the best portions of multiple takes, remove clicks, align recordings, and even reverse a recording to create a special effect.

Lessons 4–6: Working with Virtual Instruments

Lesson 4 describes how to produce virtual acoustic and electronic drummer performances using Drummer, Drum Kit Designer, and Drum Machine Designer. You will choose the right drummer for the project, swap a drum kit with the kit of another drummer, edit the patterns, change which kit elements the drummer plays, shape an interpretation, and precisely control where fills are placed.

Lessons 5 and 6 immerse you in using software instruments. After choosing virtual instruments, mapping Smart Controls to plug-in parameters, and assigning them to your MIDI controller, you'll explore MIDI recording.

Lessons 7–8: Building a Song

In Lessons 7 and 8, you'll apply Flex editing to precisely adjust the timing and pitch of notes in an audio recording. Varispeed will allow you to work with your project at different tempos. You'll add tempo changes and tempo curves to a project, match the tempos of multiple tracks with Smart Tempo, and make a track follow the groove of another track. Also covered are tuning a vocal recording, editing a project's regions in the workspace to complete an arrangement, and adding and removing sections of a project.

Lessons 9–10: Mixing and Automating a Song

Lessons 9 and 10 instruct you in mixing audio and MIDI files into a final project: adding audio effects, adjusting levels, panning, EQing, adding delay and reverb, automating the mix by creating automation curves on your screen, and altering parameter values in real time with the mouse or a MIDI controller.

Appendix A describes how to control Logic with your iPad, and Appendix B lists a wealth of useful keyboard shortcuts.

System Requirements

Before using *Apple Pro Training Series: Logic Pro X 10.4,* you should have a working knowledge of your Mac and the macOS operating system. Make sure that you know how to use the mouse and standard menus and commands; and also how to open, save, and close files. If you need to review these techniques, see the printed or online documentation included with your system.

Logic Pro X and the lessons in this book require the following system resources:

▶ Display with resolution of 1280 x 768 or higher

▶ 4 GB of RAM

▶ macOS v10.12 or later

▶ Minimum 6 GB of disk space (up to 63 GB of disk space for the full Sound Library installation)

▶ A high-speed Internet connection for installation

▶ A USB-connected MIDI keyboard (or compatible MIDI keyboard and interface) to play software instruments

▶ An audio interface (optional but recommended for audio recording)

▶ An iPhone or iPad with iOS 11 (optional) for controlling Logic using the Logic Remote iPad app

Preparing Your Logic Workstation

The exercises in this book require that you install Logic Pro X along with its default media content. If you have not yet installed Logic, you may purchase it from the App Store. When your purchase is completed, Logic Pro X will automatically be installed on your hard drive.

Some of the instructions and descriptions in this book may vary slightly depending on the sounds you have installed.

When you first open Logic Pro X, the app will automatically download and install the essential content. You may get an alert offering to download more sounds.

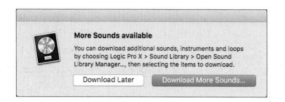

Click Download More Sounds to install all the Logic Pro X media content. After you click Download More Sounds, the Sound Library Manager window opens. Click the Select All Uninstalled button at the bottom left. Depending on the speed of your Internet connection, the download process may take several hours.

> **NOTE ▶** If you have already installed Logic Pro X but did not install the additional content, choose Logic Pro X > Sound Library > Open Sound Library Manager, and click Select All Uninstalled. (Make sure the Legacy and Compatibility content is not selected.) Then, click Install.

> **NOTE ▶** If you choose not to download the entire Logic sound library, you may be unable to find some of the media needed in the exercises. Missing media will appear dimmed with a down arrow icon. Click the down arrow icon to download that media.

Web Edition/Content Update Program

This guide is part of the Peachpit Content Update Program. When Apple updates Logic Pro, this guide may also be updated. Updates are delivered to you via a free Web Edition that contains the complete guide and all updates. When you purchase this guide from Peachpit in any format, you automatically have access to its Web Edition.

The downloadable content for *Apple Pro Training Series: Logic Pro X 10.4* includes the project files you will use for each lesson, as well as media files that contain the audio and MIDI content you will need for each exercise. After you save the files to your hard disk, each lesson will instruct you in their use.

Accessing the Lesson Files and Web Edition

When you purchase an eBook from Peachpit.com, your Web Edition automatically appears under the Digital Purchases tab on your Account page. Click the Launch link to access the product. Continue reading to learn how to register your product to get access to the lesson files.

If you purchased an eBook from a different vendor or you bought a print book, you must register your purchase on Peachpit.com to access the online content:

1   Go to www.peachpit.com/register.

2   Sign in, or create a new account.

3   Enter ISBN: 9780135244760.

4   Answer the questions as proof of purchase.

   NOTE ▶ The Web Edition will appear under the Digital Purchases tab on your Account page.

5   Click the Launch link to access the Web Edition.

6   You can access the lesson files through the Registered Products tab on your Account page. Click the Access Bonus Content link below the title of your product to proceed to the download page. Click the lesson file links to download them to your computer.

> **NOTE** ▶ If you've enabled the Desktop and your Document folder to sync to iCloud, you are strongly advised not to copy your lesson files to your Desktop. Choose another location, such as the Logic folder within your Music folder.

7   After downloading the file to your Mac desktop, you'll need to unzip the file to access a folder titled Logic Pro X Files, which you will save to your Mac desktop.

Logic Pro X Files contains two subfolders, Lessons and Media, that contain the working files for this course. Make sure you keep these two folders together in the Logic Pro X Files folder on your hard disk. If you do so, your Mac should be able to maintain the original links between the lessons and media files. Each lesson explains which files to open for that lesson's exercises.

> **MORE INFO** ▶ Access to the Web Edition doesn't automatically provide access to your lesson files, or vice versa. Follow the instructions above to claim the full benefits of your guide purchase.

Using Default Preferences and Key Commands, and Selecting the Advanced Tools

All the instructions and descriptions in this book assume that you are using the default preferences (unless instructed to change them). At the beginning of Lesson 1, you will be instructed how to show advanced tools and select all additional options.

If you have changed some of your Logic Pro X preferences, you may not realize the same results as described in the exercises. To make sure that you can follow along with this book, it's best to revert to the initial set of Logic preferences before you start the lessons. Keep in mind, however, that when you initialize preferences, you lose your custom settings, and later you may want to reset your favorite preferences manually.

1   Choose Logic Pro X > Preferences > Advanced Tools.

2   Select Show Advanced Tools.

3   Click the Enable All button to select all additional options, and then close the preferences window.

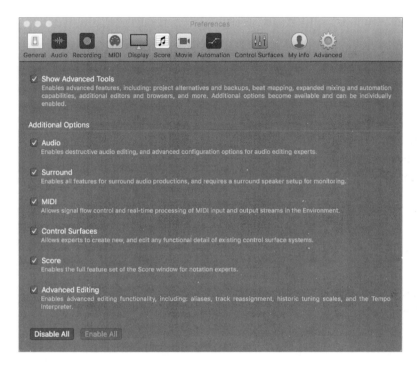

4   Choose Logic Pro X > Preferences > Reset All Preferences Except Key Commands.

A confirmation message appears.

5   Click Initialize.

Your preferences are initialized to their default states.

NOTE ▸ After initializing Preferences, you may need to re-select the desired audio interface: choose Logic Pro X > Preferences > Audio, choose your audio interface from the Output Device and Input Device pop-up menus, and make sure Core Audio is Enabled. The first time you create a new audio track, in the New Track dialog, make sure its Output is set to Output 1 + 2.

Using the U.S. Key Command Preset

This book assumes that you are using the default initialized key command preset for a U.S. keyboard. If you have customized your key commands, you may find that some of the key commands in your Logic installation do not function as they are described in this book.

If at any point you find that the key commands don't respond as described in this book, make sure the U.S. key command preset is selected on your Mac by choosing Logic Pro X > Key Commands > Presets > U.S.

Screen Resolution

Depending on your display resolution, some of the project files may appear different on your screen than they do in the book. When you open a project, if you can't see the whole Arrange window, move the window until you can see the three window controls at the left of the title bar, and click the Zoom button (the third button from the left) to fit the window to the screen.

When using a low display resolution, you may also have to zoom or scroll more often than instructed in the book when performing some of the exercise steps. In some cases, you may have to temporarily resize or close an area of the Arrange window to complete an action in another area.

About the Apple Pro Training Series

Apple Pro Training Series: Logic Pro X 10.4 is both a self-paced learning tool and the official curriculum of the Apple Pro Training and Certification Program. Developed by experts in the field and certified by Apple, the series is used by Apple Authorized Training Centers worldwide and offers complete training in all Apple Pro products. The lessons are designed to let you learn at your own pace. Each lesson concludes with review questions and answers summarizing what you've learned, which can be used to help you prepare for the Apple Pro Certification Exam.

For a complete list of Apple Pro Training Series books, see the ad at the back of this book or visit www.peachpit.com/apts.

Apple Pro Certification Program

The Apple Pro Training and Certification Program is designed to keep you at the forefront of Apple digital media technology while giving you a competitive edge in today's ever-changing job market. Whether you're an editor, graphic designer, sound designer, special-effects artist, or teacher, these training tools are meant to help you expand your skills.

Upon completing the course material in this book, you can become a certified Apple Pro by taking the certification exam at an Apple Authorized Training Center. Successful certification as an Apple Pro gives you official recognition of your knowledge of Apple professional applications while allowing you to market yourself to employers and clients as a skilled, pro-level user of Apple products.

For those who prefer to learn in an instructor-led setting, Apple offers training courses at Apple Authorized Training Centers worldwide. These courses, which use the Apple Pro Training Series books as their curriculum, are taught by Apple Certified Trainers and balance concepts and lectures with hands-on labs and exercises. Apple Authorized Training Centers have been carefully selected and have met Apple's highest standards in all areas, including facilities, instructors, course delivery, and infrastructure. The goal of the program is to offer Apple customers, from beginners to the most seasoned professionals, the highest-quality training experience.

For more information, please see the ad at the back of this book, or to find an Authorized Training Center near you, go to training.apple.com.

Resources

Apple Pro Training Series: Logic Pro X 10.4 is not intended as a comprehensive reference manual, nor does it replace the documentation that comes with the application. For comprehensive information about program features, refer to these resources:

▶ Logic Pro Help, accessed through the Logic Pro X Help menu, contains a description of most features. Other documents available in the Help menu can also be valuable resources.

▶ The Apple websites www.apple.com/logic-pro/ and www.apple.com/support/logicpro/.

▶ The official Logic Pro release notes at https://support.apple.com/en-us/HT203718/.

▶ The Logic Pro Help website, an online community of Logic users moderated by the author of this book, David Nahmani: www.logicprohelp.com/forum.

▶ For additional help with accessing the lesson files, you may send email queries to ask@peachpit.com.

Exploring the Interface and Working with Real Instruments

1

Lesson Files   None

Time   This lesson takes approximately 150 minutes to complete.

Goals   Produce a one-minute instrumental piece using prerecorded media

Explore the Logic Pro X main window interface

Navigate and zoom the workspace

Move, copy, loop, and trim regions in the workspace

Mix down the project and apply effect plug-ins

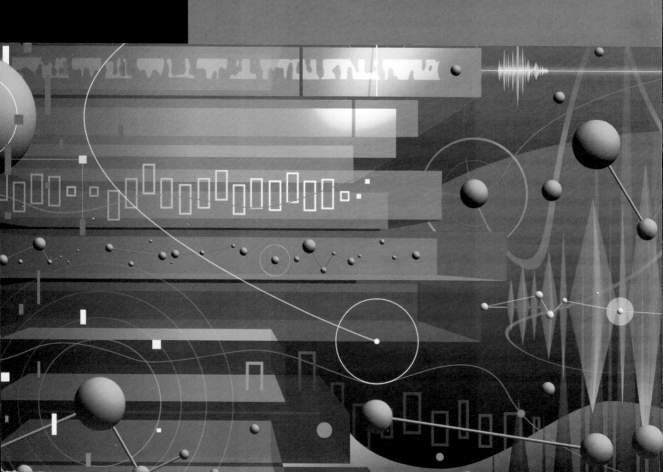

Make Music with Logic Now!

Let's get right to the heart of the matter and start producing music immediately. In this lesson, we'll go straight to the fun part of using Logic Pro X. You will create a one-minute hip-hop instrumental while gaining familiarity with Logic Pro X, its main window, and many of its features.

You will take an entire Logic project from start to finish. You'll use the Loop Browser to preview and add loops, and then you'll navigate and zoom the workspace to efficiently move, copy, loop, or trim regions. Finally, you will hone your newly learned skills to build an arrangement, mix down the song, and export it.

Creating a Logic Pro X Project

To open Logic Pro X, you can use the Launchpad.

1   In the Dock, click the Launchpad icon.

2   In the search field, type the first few letters of "Logic," and click the Logic Pro X icon.

3   If you are prompted to download additional sounds, click Download Later.

Logic Pro X opens, and after a moment, the Project Chooser opens. (If the Project Chooser does not open, close the current project, if any, then choose File > New from Template. If "New from Template" is not in the File menu, choose File > New.)

TIP ► To add Logic Pro X to the Dock, drag its icon from the Launchpad into the Dock. The next time you want to open Logic Pro X, you can click its icon in the Dock.

4   In the Project Chooser, double-click the Empty Project template.

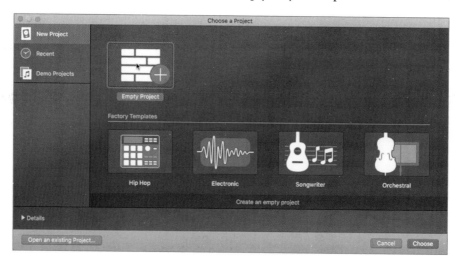

A new empty project is created, and the New Tracks dialog opens.

5   In the New Tracks dialog, select Audio (or, if you see pictures of instruments, click the picture of a microphone). Under the Details label, make sure that all checkboxes below the Input and Output menus are unselected, and then click Create (or press Return).

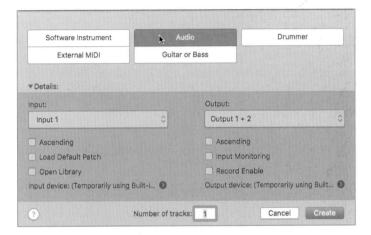

A new audio track is created in your project.

In Logic Pro X, some advanced tools may not be available by default. Before you continue, let's make sure that you select all the advanced tools in your preferences to enable all of Logic Pro X's features.

6   Choose Logic Pro X > Preferences > Advanced Tools to open the Preferences window.

7   Make sure all Additional Options are selected, and close the Preferences window.

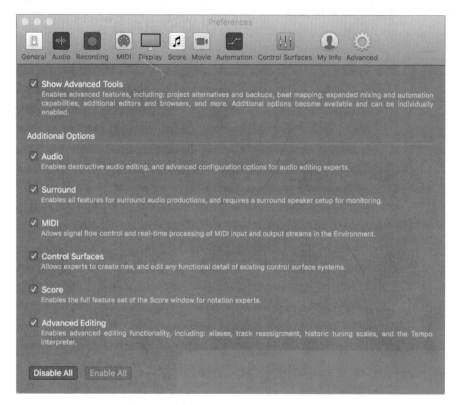

NOTE ▶ You'll have to select all the Additional Options on any Mac you use to work with this book, or you may not be able to access some of the features discussed.

Saving your project before you start working on it is always a good idea. That way you won't have to worry later about picking a name and a location when inspiration strikes.

8   Choose File > Save (or press Command-S).

You're saving this project for the first time, so a Save dialog appears. The first time you save a file, you must provide:

▶   A filename

▶   A location on the hard drive where you want to save the file

9   In the Save As field, type your project name, *Get Dancing*. From the Where pop-up menu, choose Desktop (or press Command-D).

> **NOTE ▶** If you've enabled the Desktop and your Document folder to sync to iCloud, you are strongly advised not to save your Logic projects to your Desktop. Choose another location, such as the Logic folder within your Music folder.

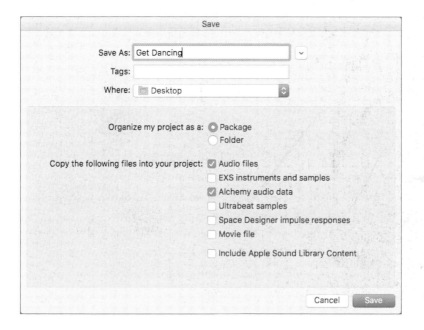

10 Click Save (or press Return).

The project is now saved on your desktop, and its name is displayed at the top of the Logic Pro X window. To avoid losing your work, save your project often.

> **NOTE ▶** Logic Pro X automatically saves your project while you're working on it. If the application unexpectedly quits, the next time you reopen the project, a dialog prompts you to reopen the most recent manually saved version or the most recent auto-saved version.

You've now set up your new project. With a blank canvas ready, you can start being creative.

Creating a new project in Logic opens the main window, which will be your main work area. In the next exercise, you will examine the panes of the main window.

Exploring the Interface

When working with Logic Pro X, you will spend most of your time in the main window. To customize the main window, you can toggle and resize its various panes to access all the media, tools, and features you need for your project.

Control bar

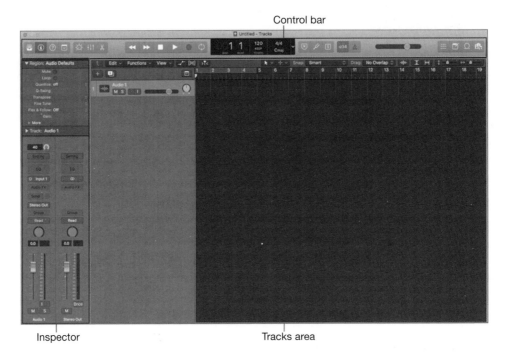

Inspector   Tracks area

In its default configuration, the main window has three areas:

▶ Control bar—The control bar contains buttons to toggle areas on and off; transport buttons to control playback operations (such as play, stop, rewind, and forward); information displays to indicate the playhead position, project tempo, time, and key signatures; and mode buttons such as Count-in and Metronome.

▶ Inspector—The inspector provides access to a contextual set of parameters. The specific parameters displayed depend on the selected track or region, or the area in key focus.

▶ Tracks area—In the Tracks area you build your song by arranging regions on tracks located below a ruler.

Customizing your main window layout to display the tools you need allows you to work faster and more comfortably, thereby giving you more time to focus on your music.

1   In the control bar, click the Inspector button (or press I).

The inspector is hidden, which allows you to see more of the Tracks area.

2   Click the Toolbar button (or press Control-Option-Command-T).

The toolbar opens below the control bar. It displays buttons for easy access to the most-used features.

TIP ▶ To customize the control bar, Control-click it, and from the shortcut menu, choose "Customize Control Bar and Display." To customize the toolbar, Control-click it and choose Customize Toolbar.

3   Click the Quick Help button.

Yellow help tags appear. As you hover the mouse pointer over elements of the Logic Pro X interface, help tags appear that describe that element.

4   In the toolbar, position the mouse pointer over the Track Zoom button.

A help tag displays the function's name, defines what it does, and sometimes offers extra information. Whenever you're not sure what an interface element does, use Quick Help.

MORE INFO ▶ To go further, read the Logic Pro Help documentation within the free Logic Remote iPad app. The documentation automatically displays the section relevant to the Logic Pro X area where you place the mouse pointer. You will learn more about Logic Remote in Appendix A.

5   Click the Quick Help button to close the Quick Help window.

6   Click the Toolbar button to close the toolbar.

7   Click the Mixer button (or press X).

The Mixer opens below the Tracks area.

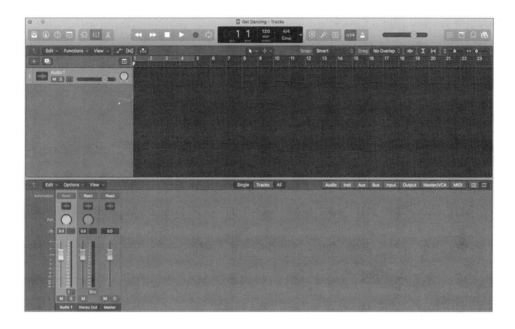

8   After viewing the tools in the Mixer, click the Mixer button again (or press X) to close it.

9   In the control bar, click the Apple Loops button (or press O).

Apple Loops button

The Loop Browser opens to the right of the Tracks area.

NOTE ▶ The first time you open the Loop Browser, you have to wait for Logic to index the loops before you can use it.

You now have the control bar at the top, the Tracks area to the left, and the Loop Browser to the right, which is the perfect layout for the next exercise.

You're already gaining familiarity with the Logic Pro X interface. By showing only those panes needed for the task at hand, you make your work easier and faster, allowing you to focus on the creative side. And talking about creative side, let's make some music!

Adding Apple Loops

You will now start building your project using Apple Loops, which are prerecorded music snippets that automatically match the tempo of your project and are designed to be repeated seamlessly.

Professional producers use Apple Loops all the time for video soundtracks, to add texture to a beat, to create unexpected effects, and so on. At least one major hit song was produced entirely around a single Apple Loop. The Apple Loops included with Logic Pro X (and earlier versions of Logic) are royalty free, so you can use them in professional projects without worrying about licensing rights.

Browsing and Previewing Loops

To start building this song, you need to preview loops and choose which ones to use. The Loop Browser is the perfect tool for this job. It allows you to browse loops by instrument, genre, mood, and other attributes.

NOTE ▶ Depending on the Logic content installed on your Mac, some loops may not yet be downloaded and appear dimmed. You can click the button to the right of any dimmed loop name to download and install the Loop Pack that contains that loop.

1   In the Loop Browser, click the Instrument button, and then click the All Drums keyword button.

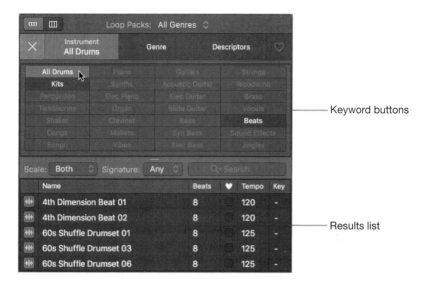

Keyword buttons

Results list

A broad search such as this one will return a lot of results, so you will now narrow the search.

2   Click the Descriptors button, and then click the Acoustic and Distorted keyword buttons.

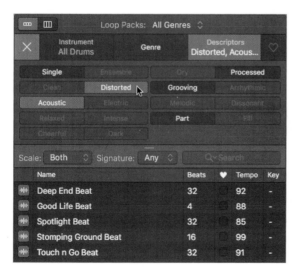

Each time you click a keyword button, the results list is shortened because fewer loops match the narrowing keyword search.

You can preview loops by clicking them.

3   In the results list, click the first loop, **Deep End Beat**.

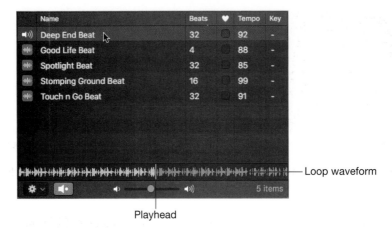

Loop waveform

Playhead

The loop is selected, its blue loop icon turns into a speaker, and the loop plays. When a loop is playing, its waveform is displayed at the bottom of the Loop browser. To preview different sections of the loop, you can click anywhere on the waveform to move the playhead. At any time, you can click another loop to preview it, or click the currently playing loop to stop playback.

In the control bar, the information display shows the default project tempo of 120 bpm (beats per minute). When a project is empty, Apple Loops are previewed at their original tempos. Once a region is present in a project, Apple Loops are previewed at the project tempo.

Tempo

In the results list, you can see that **Deep End Beat** was produced at a tempo of 92 bpm. Loops usually work best when used at or near their original tempos, so let's change the project tempo.

TIP ▸ You can change numerical values in Logic Pro X two ways: drag the value up or down to increase or decrease it, or double-click the value and enter the desired number.

4   In the control bar's LCD display, drag the tempo value down to 92 bpm.

5   Click the loop to stop playback, and click it again to resume playback at the new tempo.

The loop plays back at the 92 bpm project tempo. The loop does seem to groove better at the slower tempo.

6   Further down, click **Good Life Beat**, to preview it at the project tempo of 92 bpm.

This loop has a nice funky feel, and you are going to use it as the beat for your music project.

7   Drag **Good Life Beat** from the results list to track 1 in the workspace, making sure the help tag reads *Position: 1 1 1 1*.

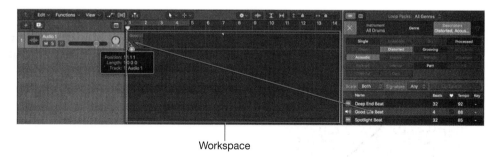

Workspace

The workspace is the area below the ruler and to the right of the track headers, where regions are arranged to build a song.

The loop is imported, and an audio region is placed on the audio track at the very beginning of the project. An alert asks if you would like to use the tempo information embedded in the loop. The Loop Browser shows that the **Good Life Beat** original tempo is 88 bpm, a little slower than your current 92 bpm tempo. You will use that new tempo.

8   Click Import (or press Return).

In the control bar's LCD display, the project tempo changes to the tempo of the loop. (The displayed tempo may be rounded off by 1 bpm.)

9   Choose File > Save (or press Command-S).

Your project now contains a single drum loop on a single track that plays only during bar 1. It's the most basic project, just enough for you to dive into the basic tasks of positioning the playhead, and starting and stopping playback. Later you will use those navigation chops to preview bass lines while listening to your new drum region and add more loops.

Navigating the Project

One of the big advantages to producing music with a computer is that the whole song is laid out right before your eyes. This representation makes it extremely easy to jump to a specific part of the song, start playback, quickly return to the beginning, or continuously repeat a section.

Logic offers many ways to navigate your project. In the following two exercises, you will use the transport buttons and their key commands, and you will learn how to continuously repeat a section of the project, which will allow you to keep playing the drum loop while you preview bass loops.

Using Transport Buttons and Key Commands

When you're producing music, time is of the essence. Because many producing tasks are repetitive, you may find yourself playing, stopping, and positioning the playhead every few seconds. Minimizing the time it takes to perform these basic operations will greatly improve your workflow and save valuable time.

Although you may initially find it easier to click transport buttons with the mouse, moving a mouse with your hand while keeping your eyes on the screen is actually a time-consuming task. Using key commands to control playback can significantly reduce that time, increasing your workflow efficiency as your fingers build up muscle memory.

To fully master key commands, you first need to understand *key focus*, which determines the pane of the main window that will respond to key commands. To start this next exercise, you will preview an Apple Loop to make sure your Loop Browser has key focus.

1   In the Loop Browser results list, click any loop to preview it.

2   Click that same loop again to stop it.

Notice the blue frame around the Loop Browser. It indicates that the Loop Browser has key focus and is ready to respond to all Loop Browser key commands. Only one area at a time can have key focus.

3   Press Option-Spacebar (the Preview key command).

In the Loop Browser, the selected loop starts playing.

4   Press Option-Spacebar again to stop playing the loop.

Now let's give key focus to the Tracks area.

5   Click the background of the workspace (or press Tab).

The blue frame appears around the Tracks area to show that the Tracks area has key focus.

> **TIP** ▶ When multiple panes are open in the main window, you can press Tab and Shift-Tab to cycle the key focus forward and backward through the panes.

6   Press Option-Spacebar.

In the Tracks area, the playhead starts moving, playback begins, and during bar 1, you can hear the drum region on your track. The Tracks area has key focus, so the project starts playing back rather than playing the loop selected in the Loop Browser. When a key command, such as the Preview key command, could have an effect on multiple open panes, the pane that has key focus is the one that responds.

To navigate your project, you can also click the transport buttons in the control bar.

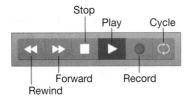

7   In the control bar, click the Stop button (or press the Spacebar).

The playhead stops, and the Stop button is replaced with a Go to Beginning button.

8   Click the Go to Beginning button (or press Return) to return the playhead to the beginning of the project.

9   Click the Forward button, or press . (period) a few times.

The playhead jumps one bar forward each time.

10   Click the Rewind button, or press , (comma) a few times.

The playhead jumps one bar backward each time.

> **TIP** ▶ To fast-forward eight bars at a time, press Shift-. (period); to fast-rewind eight bars at a time, press Shift-, (comma).

You can also position the playhead precisely where you want it by clicking in the ruler.

11 In the lower half of the ruler, click bar 5 to move the playhead to that location.

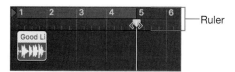

To start or stop playback at a specific location, you can double-click the lower half of the ruler.

12 Double-click the lower half of the ruler at bar 3.

Playback starts from bar 3. You can also position the playhead without interrupting playback.

13 Without stopping playback, click the lower half of the ruler at bar 1.

You can again hear your drum loop.

14 Double-click in the lower-half of the ruler.

Playback stops and the playhead moves to the location you clicked.

Continuously Repeating a Section

Sometimes when you are working on a specific section of your project, you may want to repeat a section multiple times without stopping playback. As you're working, the beat keeps going, and you no longer have to manually relocate the playhead.

You will continue building your project by adding a bass track. To determine which bass loop works best with your drums, you will use Cycle mode to continuously repeat bar 1 as you preview bass loops in the Loop Browser.

You need to adjust the cycle area so that it spans the same length as the drum region. To do so, you will first select the drum region, which was deselected in the previous exercise when you clicked the background of the workspace.

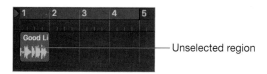

1   Click the drum region.

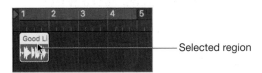

────────── Selected region

The region is highlighted to indicate that it is selected.

2   Choose Navigate > Set Rounded Locators by Selection and Enable Cycle (or press U).

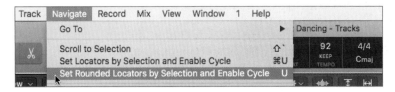

TIP ▶ When choosing a menu command, the corresponding key command usually appears to the right.

In the control bar, the Cycle button is turned on, and in the ruler, the cycle area turns yellow, indicating that Cycle mode is enabled.

Left locator   Right locator

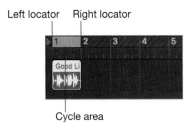

Cycle area

The cycle area shows the section of the song that will repeat. The start and end position of the cycle area, called left and right locators, match the start and end of the selected region, and the cycle area goes from bar 1 to bar 2. When you choose "Set Rounded Locators by Selection and Enable Cycle," the locators are always rounded to the nearest bar, so repeating the cycle area keeps the groove going.

3   Press the Spacebar to start playback.

The playhead starts moving, and your drums play. When the playhead reaches bar 2, it immediately jumps back to the beginning of bar 1 and continues playback.

While your drums continue playing, you can preview some bass loops.

4   In the Loop Browser, at the top left, click the X button.

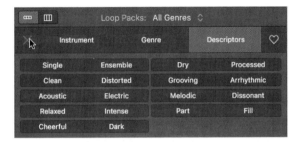

All keyword buttons are disabled.

For the bass loops, let's limit the search to a specific musical genre.

5   At the top of the Loop Browser, from the Loop Packs pop-up menu, choose Hip Hop.

Only loops from the Hip Hop collection are displayed in the results list.

6   Click the Instrument button, then click the Bass keyword button.

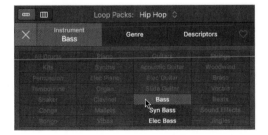

Since we know loops typically work better when played close to their original tempos, let's sort the results list by tempo and look for loops that were produced at or around 88 bpm.

7   At the top of the results list, click the Tempo column name.

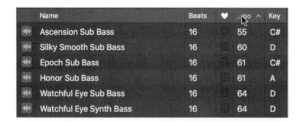

	Name	Beats	♥	po ^	Key
⦀	Ascension Sub Bass	16		55	C#
⦀	Silky Smooth Sub Bass	16		60	D
⦀	Epoch Sub Bass	16		61	C#
⦀	Honor Sub Bass	16		61	A
⦀	Watchful Eye Sub Bass	16		64	D
⦀	Watchful Eye Synth Bass	16		64	D

The loops in the results list are sorted by increasing tempo.

8   Scroll down to see loops with a tempo of 88 bpm.

9   Click the first loop with a tempo of 88 bpm.

After a moment, Logic syncs the loop with the project and you can hear it playing, grooving along with the drums in your project.

10   Continue clicking the following loops to preview them one by one.

Most of them are too synthetic for this project, but **Skyline Bass** seems to have the right sound and it works with your drums. With an original tempo of 90 bpm, it's still very close to your project tempo, which means it should work great.

Skyline Bass is listed in the results list as a 16 beats loop, but right now your cycle area is playing only one bar (at the current 4/4 time signature, 1 bar = 4 beats), so you're hearing only a portion of the bass loop. Let's add it to the project to audition the entire loop.

11   In the control bar, click the Stop button (or press the Spacebar) to stop playback.

12   Drag **Skyline Bass** to the workspace below the drum loop, making sure the help tag reads 1 1 1 1.

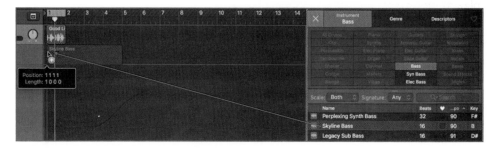

A new track is automatically created for the new *Skyline Bass* region.

13 In the ruler, click the yellow cycle area to turn off Cycle mode (or press C).

14 In the control bar, click the Go to Beginning button (or press Return).

15 Press the Spacebar to start playback.

In the first bar, you can hear both the drum loop and the bass loop; then the drums drop off while the bass continues playing for three more bars. You can now hear the entire bass line, which is even more melodic than the limited preview you heard previously.

16 Press the Spacebar again to stop playback.

17 Choose File > Save (or press Command-S).

As you work in Logic, keep saving your project at regular intervals to avoid losing any of your work.

Setting locators to adjust the cycle area is a technique you'll use often throughout your production to focus on part of a project. And if you work with other musicians in your studio, they will love you for not interrupting the playback (and ruining their creative flow) every few bars!

Building Up the Rhythm Section

All the material you use for a project is contained in regions that are on tracks in the workspace. Creating an arrangement is a little like playing with building blocks—moving, copying, or repeating regions as needed to determine at which points specific instruments start and stop playing.

In this exercise, you will start building an arrangement with the drum and bass loops, and later add more loops to complete your project. First, you will loop both regions so they play continuously.

1 In the control bar, click the Inspector button (or press I).

The inspector appears. Region parameters for the selected region(s) are displayed in the Region inspector near the top.

2   In the workspace, click the *Good Life Beat* region in track 1 to select it.

The Region inspector shows the parameters of the *Good Life Beat* region.

3   In the Region inspector, select the Loop checkbox (or press L).

In the workspace, *Good Life Beat* is now looping until the end of the project.

4   In the workspace, click the bass region in track 2 to select it.

5   In the Region inspector, select the Loop checkbox.

In the workspace, both the drum and the bass regions are now looping.

6   Listen to a few bars of the project.

The drums and bass are grooving together perfectly. You're going to layer the drums with an urban percussion loop that will also help create a nice little intro.

TIP To work more efficiently, remember to hide those areas you don't need to see. For the next few exercises, in the control bar, click the Inspector button (or press I) and click the Apple Loops button (or press O) to turn those two areas on and off as needed.

7   At the top of the Loop Browser, from the Loops pop-up menu, choose All Genres.

All keyword buttons are reset.

8   In the Loop Browser, click the search box and type *Fine*.

9   From the results list, drag **Fine Line Beat** to bar 1 below the two tracks in the workspace.

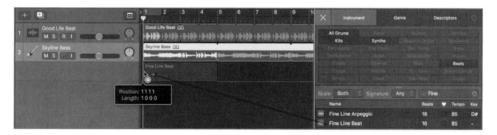

A new track is created for the *Fine Line Beat* region. Since *Fine Line Beat* is still selected, you can access its region parameters at the top of the inspector.

10   In the *Fine Line Beat* region parameters, select the Loop checkbox (or press L).

The *Fine Line Beat* region is now looping in the workspace. Since *Fine Line Beat* will be used for the intro, you can move it to the top of the workspace.

11 In the *Fine Line Beat* track header, click-hold the track icon and drag up until the two other tracks move down.

The tracks are reordered with the new *Fine Line Beat* track at the top.

To create an intro in which only *Fine Line Beat* is playing, you'll move the two other regions farther to the right. To select multiple regions at once, you can click in the workspace background and drag the pointer over the regions.

12 In the workspace, click the background, and drag up to select both the *Good Life Beat* and *Skyline Bass* regions.

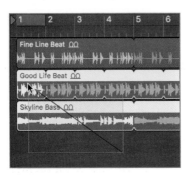

Both regions are highlighted to indicate that they're selected. You can now move them both at the same time.

13 Make sure you click one of the selected regions (don't click one of the loops to their right), and drag to bar 5.

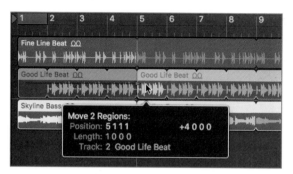

If you clicked *Good Life Beat*, the help tag shows:

▶ Move 2 Regions—The action you're performing.

▶ Position: 5 1 1 1—Where the regions are moved.

▶ +4 0 0 0—The regions are moved exactly 4 bars later.

▶ Length: 1 0 0 0—Length of the clicked region.

▶ Track: 2 Good Life Beat—Track number and name of the clicked region.

The help tag displays positions and lengths in bars, beats, divisions, and ticks. You will often refer to a position or a length with those four numbers.

▶ The bar consists of several beats (four beats in the 4/4 time signature here).

▶ The beat is the denominator in the time signature (quarter note here).

▶ The division determines how the grid is subdivided in the ruler when zoomed in horizontally (sixteenth note here).

▶ A clock tick is 1/960 of a quarter note. A sixteenth note contains 240 ticks.

Note that by default, in the control bar, the LCD displays the position of the playhead using only the first two units, bars and beats.

14 Listen to your project from the beginning.

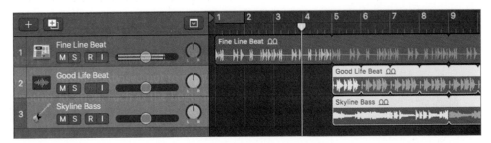

It's time to practice your navigation chops! You can click the Play and Stop/Go to Beginning buttons in the control bar, click and double-click the lower half of the ruler, or use the following key commands:

Spacebar	Play/Stop
Return	Go to beginning
. (period)	Forward
, (comma)	Rewind

The intro sounds good, and the layered drum loops work great together. However, *Good Life Beat* is a bit too loud.

15 If tracks 2 and 3 are still selected, click one of their instrument icons to deselect one track.

Having a single track selected ensures you're not affecting multiple tracks when making an adjustment.

16 In the *Good Life Beat* track header (track 2), drag the volume slider to the left to turn down the volume to about –8.0 dB.

Now the two drum loops blend together.

Near the end of this lesson, you will spend more time mixing the song, but for now let's continue editing regions and adding more loops to continue the arrangement.

Zooming In to Edit the Intro

Your project starts with a 4-bar intro in which only the *Fine Line Beat* region on track 1 plays the beat. It feels sparse, but the beat is original enough to capture attention, which is the role of an intro. Then at bar 5 both the *Good Life Beat* and *Skyline Bass* regions on tracks 2 and 3 come in, making the beat sound complete and introducing the melody.

To accentuate the starting impact of the two new regions, you will create a couple of unexpected edits at the end of the intro that are bound to make the listener's head turn. To be able to edit the *Fine Line Beat* region in the intro without affecting its loops to the right, you first have to copy the region to bar 5.

1 Option-drag the *Fine Line Beat* region to bar 5.

When Option-dragging to copy regions, always make sure you release the mouse button first and the Option key last. If you try to release both at the same time, you may sometimes release the Option key slightly before the mouse button without noticing, and then the region is moved instead of copied.

If you copied the *Fine Line Beat* region successfully, your workspace will look like this:

If you don't see a *Fine Line Beat* region between bars 1 and 5, you've moved the region rather than copying it. To reverse your last action, choose Edit > Undo Drag, and then try again.

The new *Fine Line Beat.1* region at bar 5 currently stops the original *Fine Line Beat* region at bar 1 from looping. However, the region's Loop parameter is still on, so its loops reappear if there's room for them on the track. To create a break, you need to stop the region from looping.

2   Click the *Fine Line Beat* region at bar 1 to select it.

3   In the inspector, deselect the Loop checkbox (or press L).

To create a break in the beat at the end of the intro, you will shorten the *Fine Line Beat* region so that it doesn't play the last two notes of the region. To resize the region comfortably, you need to zoom in until you can clearly see the individual drum hits on the waveform.

To use the zoom tool, you hold down Control and Option and then drag the area you want to magnify. The size of the area you drag determines how far you will zoom in: the smaller the area that you drag, the closer you'll zoom in.

4   Control-Option-drag a small blue highlight rectangle about one bar wide, but straddling the junction of the two regions on track 1 at bar 5.

The area you highlighted expands to fill the workspace, and you can clearly see individual drum hits on the waveform.

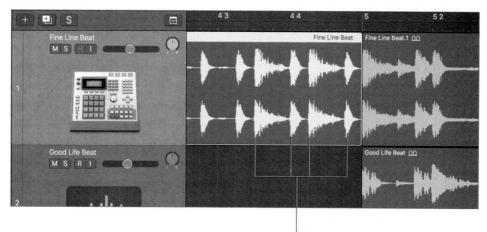

Individual drum hits

Zooming in and out efficiently to see exactly what you need takes practice. If you're not happy with what you're seeing in your workspace, Control-Option-click the workspace to zoom back out, and try again.

TIP ▶ If you're happy with your workspace view but feel that you should zoom in even closer, zoom in again. You can Control-Option-drag to zoom in multiple times and Control-Option-click the workspace multiple times to zoom back out through the same zoom levels.

To create the break at the end of the *Fine Line Beat* region, you will drag its lower-right corner to the left until the final two drum hits are hidden.

5   Move the mouse pointer over the lower-right corner of the *Fine Line Beat* region (the mouse pointer should be located just before bar 5).

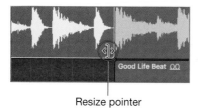

Resize pointer

The mouse pointer turns into a Resize pointer you can drag to determine where the region stops playing.

6 Drag the Resize pointer to the left to hide the final two drum hits.

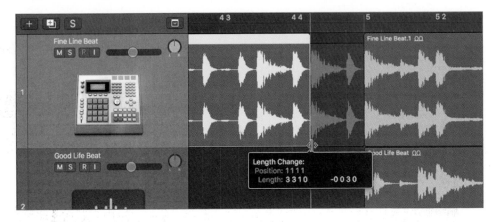

7 Control-Option-click the workspace to zoom out.

8 Listen to the song from the beginning.

The drum break creates a sudden void at the end of the intro, which reinforces the impact of the drums and bass. But a void calls out to be filled! That break in the drum loop is the perfect time to capture the attention of the listener by introducing the bass a few notes earlier.

This time you will copy the bass region from bar 5 to bar 1, and resize the bass region in the intro from the left so it plays only the final few notes.

9 On track 3, Option-drag the *Skyline Bass* region to bar 1.

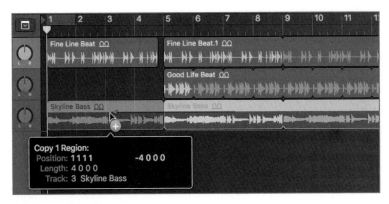

10   In the new *Skyline Bass.1* Region inspector, deselect the Loop checkbox (or press L).

This time you will use the Z key to zoom in and out of the selection.

11   Press Z.

The *Skyline Bass.1* region expands to fill the workspace.

12   Move the mouse pointer over the lower-left corner of the region, and drag the Resize pointer to the right, leaving only the last group of five notes.

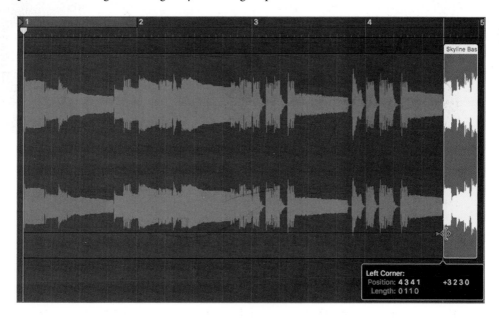

13   Click the background of the workspace to deselect all regions.

When there's no selection, pressing the Z key shows you all the regions in your workspace.

14   Press Z.

The workspace zooms out to display all the regions. It doesn't allow for the regions' loops. You can use zoom sliders or key commands to fine-tune the zoom level.

15 At the top of the workspace, drag the horizontal zoom slider to the left (or press Command-Left Arrow).

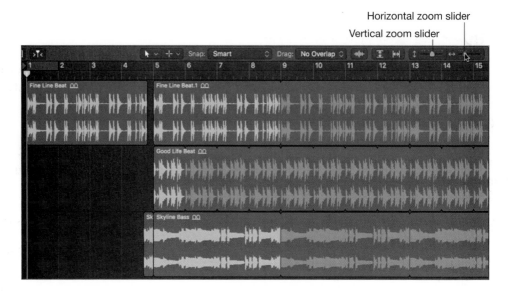

The workspace zooms out horizontally, and you can see a few more bars in your ruler.

NOTE ▶ When zooming horizontally using the zoom sliders or Command-Arrow key combinations, the playhead stays at the same position on your screen, unless a region is selected and the playhead is not within that region's borders. In that case, the left edge of the region stays at the same position on your screen. When the play-head is offscreen, the content to the left of the workspace stays at the same position on your screen.

When zooming vertically with the zoom sliders or Command-Arrow keys, the selected region stays at the same position on your screen. If no regions are selected, the selected track stays at the same position on your screen.

16 Play your new intro.

It works! You start with an original but commanding beat with kicks and handclaps—then all of a sudden, the bass announces the melody with a few pickup notes while the beat drops. On the first beat of the next bar, all three tracks play the entire groove together. That little break at the end of the intro really calls attention to the layered drum and bass groove that starts after the intro.

Remember your newly acquired navigation and zooming skills. You will continue using them to finish this arrangement, and throughout the rest of this book (and long after).

Build Up the Arrangement

Now that you have the rhythmic foundation of your project (the drums and bass), you can continue building up the arrangement and avoid monotony by adding melodic elements.

Adding Lead Synths

In the next exercise, you will add a couple of synth arpeggio loops. And rather than let them loop throughout the song, you will keep things moving by alternating between the two synth melodies.

1   In the Loop Browser, click the X symbol in the search field to clear the previous search.

   You already have a solid rhythmic section with bass and low kick drums, so now you are looking for rather clean and high-pitched sounds.

2   Click the Instrument button, and then click the Synths keyword button.

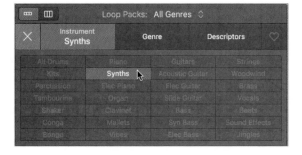

3   In the search field, type *arpeggio*.

4   In the results list, click the Name column title to reorder the results by loop name.

5   In the results list, click the first few loops to preview them.

Two loops fit the bill perfectly: **Barricade Arpeggio** and **Deal Breaker Arpeggio**. If necessary, adjust the zoom level in the workspace so you can comfortably drag both loops
to two new tracks.

6   Drag the **Barricade Arpeggio** loop to the bottom of the workspace at bar 9.

7   Drag the **Deal Breaker Arpeggio** loop to the bottom of the workspace at bar 10.

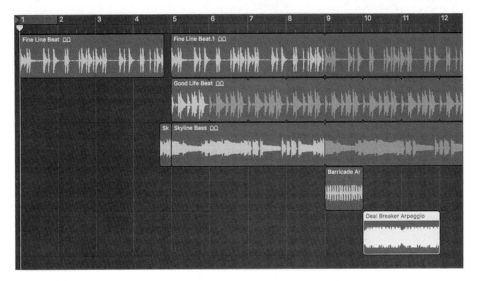

You will resize the *Deal Breaker Arpeggio* region to make it one bar long, the same
length as the *Barricade Arpeggio* region.

8   Drag the lower-right corner of the *Deal Breaker Arpeggio* region to make it one bar long.

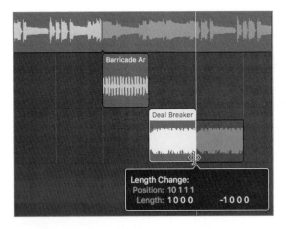

You will now copy both regions so they play alternately.

9   Drag a rectangle around both regions to select them.

10   Choose Edit > Repeat (or press Command-R).

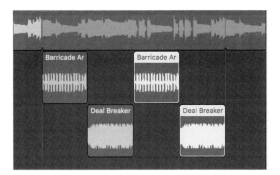

11   Play the new synth section.

The two synths bring much-needed melody and movement to the song, and they work well in answering each other, each one successively playing its melody.

Currently, both synths sound as if they are coming from the center of the stereo field. To give them a little space, you can spread them apart acoustically by positioning them to either side of the stereo field.

If tracks are selected automatically when you select regions on those tracks, you can change this behavior in Logic preferences.

12   Choose Logic Pro X > Preferences > General, click the Edit tab, and make sure "Select tracks on region selection" is deselected.

13 Click the synth icon on one of the selected tracks to deselect the other track.

14 In the workspace, drag a selection rectangle around multiple regions.

The track selection is unaffected by the region selection.

15 On the *Barricade Arpeggio* track header, click the Pan knob and drag down to turn the knob to the left.

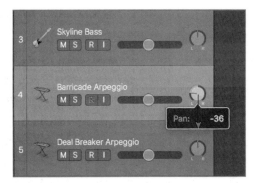

16 On the *Deal Breaker Arpeggio* track, click the Pan knob and drag up to turn it to the right.

17 Play the synth section again.

You can now hear the two synths playing from opposite sides of the stereo field, which adds dimension to the music and helps separate the two instruments.

Creating a Break

Until now, you have kept your project interesting by introducing new elements on a regular basis: the bass at the end of the intro, the drums at bar 5, a synth at bar 9, and another synth at bar 10. But if you keep building your song by adding more elements, at some point those additions may backfire. The song can become bloated, with the arrangement losing focus, the mix becoming muddy, and the listeners tuning out. Who wants that?

So, if you can't add any more to your song, subtract! By the end of the new synth section, the listeners are so used to hearing the drums and the bass that they may no longer pay attention to them. If you remove them, you can create a big impact. So, let's add a piano loop after the synth section, and then delete the drums and bass while the piano plays.

At the top of the Tracks area, look at the tool menus:

The menu to the left corresponds to the tool assigned to the mouse pointer.

The menu to the right corresponds to the tool assigned to the mouse pointer when holding down Command.

Currently, the left-click tool is assigned to the Pointer tool (arrow icon) and the Command-click tool is assigned to the Marquee tool (crosshair icon). You don't need to change those assignments; but if you're curious, feel free to click one of the tool menus to open it and see what's available. Click it again to close it.

The Loop Browser sometimes shows multiple loops with similar names, and that usually means that the loops all follow the same groove, they all follow the same chord progression, or they are meant to work together. Let's see if you have any other Skyline Apple Loops meant to work with your **Skyline Bass** loop.

1   In the Loop Browser, click the Reset button to clear all keyword buttons.

2   In the search field, type *Skyline*.

   The results list shows loops containing *Skyline* in their names.

3   Preview a few of the loops in the result list.

The loops sound like they would all work great together because they all follow the same harmony and rhythm.

4   Drag the Skyline Piano loop to the bottom of the workspace at bar 13.

You will now create the break by deleting the drums in track 2 and the bass in track 3 for the entire time the piano is playing.

5   Hold down the Command key to turn the mouse pointer into a Marquee tool.

6   Command-drag around tracks 2 and 3 from bar 13 to bar 17.

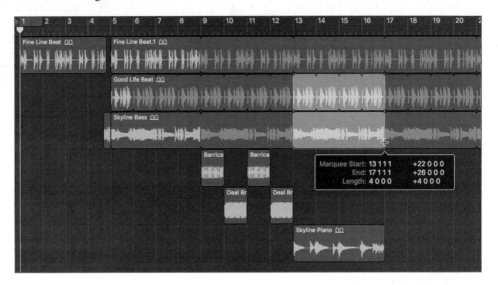

The Marquee tool places a white highlight rectangle around the selected section of the loops.

7 Choose Edit > Delete (or press Delete).

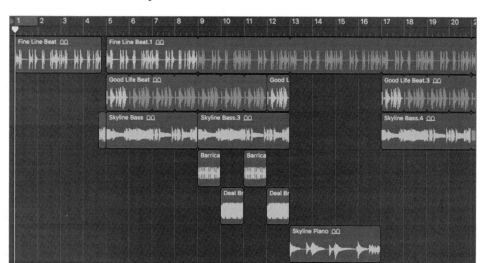

The section of the loops selected by the Marquee tool is deleted. Some loops are turned into regions before and after the empty space, so the tracks stop and resume playing at the beginning and end of the removed section.

Let's finish the song. You will let the rhythm section play four bars after the piano stops, and you'll end the song at bar 21.

8 Move the mouse pointer to the upper part of the loops on track 1.

The mouse pointer turns into a Loop tool. You can click or drag the Loop tool where you want a region's loops to end. Dragging offers the advantage of seeing the exact position in a help tag.

9   Drag the Loop tool to bar 21.

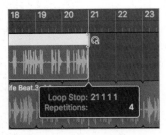

The *Fine Line Beat.1* region stops looping at bar 21.

10   Repeat the same process to stop the drums on track 2 and the bass on track 3 at bar 21.

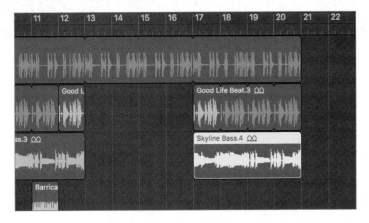

11   Move the playhead to bar 11 and press the Spacebar to play through the break and ending.

The break brings much needed space and silence, interrupts the flow of the rhythmic section, and automatically shines a light on the two remaining elements: the drum loop and the piano. After the break, the rhythmic section resumes, but the ending at bar 21 is too abrupt. Let's bring back the piano by itself to create a quick outro.

12   On track 6, Option-drag the *Skyline Piano* region to bar 21.

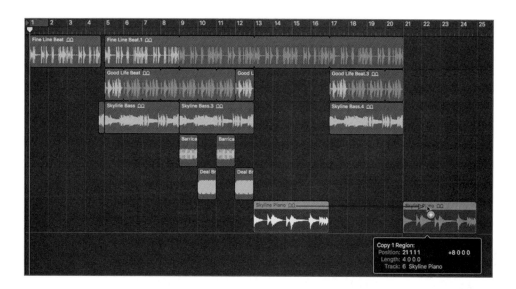

You will finally shorten the new copy of the piano region so it ends with a sustaining note, which will work better for an ending.

13 Control-Option-drag around the *Skyline Piano.1* region to zoom in on it.

14 Drag the lower-right corner of the *Skyline Piano.1* region to the left so that it ends with the long sustaining note in bar 23.

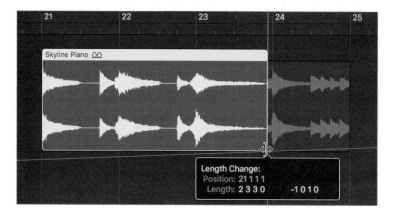

15 Control-Option-click the workspace to zoom out.

16 Play the entire project.

You have arranged your first song. Using only six Apple Loops, you've built a simple one-minute song that evolves from an original intro into a solid bass and drums groove. Then two synths share the lead melody for a few bars before the bass and drums abruptly stop to leave room for a piano break. Finally, the bass and drums groove returns, and the song finishes with a few sustained piano notes. Really nice! You will now quickly mix the song and later export it to share it.

Mixing the Song

Now that you have arranged your regions in the workspace, you can focus on the sound of each instrument and how they sound as an ensemble. You can adjust each instrument's loudness and its position in the stereo field, and even modify its timbre so all the instruments blend harmoniously.

Choosing Names and Icons for Tracks and Channel Strips

You will open the Mixer and name your channel strips so you can easily determine which instrument they control. You will then adjust the Volume faders and Pan knobs to change levels and stereo positions, and use plug-ins to process some of the instruments.

1   In the control bar, click the Mixer button (or press X).

At the bottom of the main window, the Mixer opens.

The channel strips are named after the Apple Loops that you previously dragged to the workplace. To more quickly locate instruments, you can assign the channel strips more descriptive names.

To edit the name on a track header and on its corresponding channel strip, you can double-click either and type the new name.

2   At the bottom of the first channel strip, double-click the *Fine Line Beat* name.

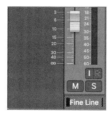

A text entry box appears, and the current name—*Fine Line Beat*—is selected.

3   Type *Beat Loop*, and press Return.

Both the first channel strip in the Mixer and track 1 in the Tracks area are renamed *Beat Loop*. Renaming tracks in the track header is often easier because you can quickly identify instruments by looking at the regions you've been arranging.

4   In the control bar, click the Mixer button again (or press X) to close the Mixer.

5   In track 2's track header, double-click the *Good Life Beat* name.

A text entry box opens. This time you will enter a name and open the text entry box of the next track with a single key command.

6   Type *Drums*, and press Tab.

Track 2 is renamed *Drums*. A text entry box opens on track 3's name, ready to be edited.

7 Type *Bass*, and press Tab.

Track 3 is renamed *Bass*, and track 4 is ready to be renamed.

8 Type *Synth 1*, and press Tab.

9 Type *Synth 2*, and press Tab.

10 Type *Piano*, and press Return.

> **TIP** In the Mixer, you can also press Tab to enter a name and open the text entry box of the next channel strip. Should you enter a name incorrectly, press Shift-Tab to open the text entry box of the previous track or channel strip.

Notice that track 2 has only a generic audio waveform icon. That's because the track was created before you dragged the **Good Life Beat** loop to it at the very beginning of this lesson.

11 In the Tracks area, Control-click the icon in track 2's track header.

A shortcut menu displays icons organized in categories.

12 In the shortcut menu, click the Drums category.

A collection of various drum icons appears.

13 Click an icon representing a drum kit.

The icon is now visible in the track header. The same icon is also assigned to the corresponding channel strip in the Mixer, as you will see in a moment.

When your creative juices are flowing, and you just want to make a quick adjustment to the sound of an instrument, wasting time looking for the correct track or channel strip can be frustrating. Or worse, you could become a victim of the classic mistake: turning knobs and faders but not hearing the sound reacting to your adjustments, until you realize you were adjusting the wrong instrument!

Taking a minute to assign your tracks and channel strips descriptive names and appropriate icons can accelerate your workflow and avoid potentially costly mistakes.

Adjusting Volume and Stereo Position

With new names and icons assigned, your Mixer is ready. You will now open it and adjust some of the instruments' volume levels and stereo positions.

1 In the control bar, click the Mixer button (or press X) to open the Mixer.

You can see your new names at the bottom of the channel strips. You can resize the Mixer area to see more of the channel strips.

2 Place the mouse pointer between the Tracks area and the Mixer area.

A Resize pointer appears.

3   Drag the Resize pointer up as far as it will go.

The Mixer is now taller, and you can see more options at the top of the channel strips. There are a lot of options, but don't worry. Just because you have many tools available doesn't mean you have to use them all. You will learn about those options as needed.

NOTE ▶ Depending on the size of your display, you may not be able to open up the Mixer all the way. In that case, you can drag the vertical scrollbar to the right of the Mixer to scroll up and see all the options.

4   Play your song.

With the Mixer open and occupying most of the main window, the workspace is much smaller. Depending on your display resolution, navigating your song efficiently may prove challenging (or nearly impossible). To remedy that, you will now adjust the locators in the Tracks area ruler and use Cycle mode to continuously repeat a part of the song that contains all the instruments.

5   Click the Mixer button (or press X) to close the Mixer.

If necessary, scroll or zoom out in the workspace so you can see your entire arrangement. Remember: to see all your regions, click the background of the workspace and press Z.

6   Drag the upper half of the ruler from bar 9 to bar 13.

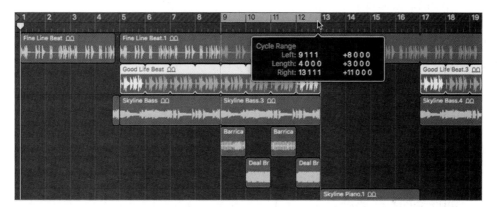

Cycle mode is turned on, and a cycle area appears where you dragged. The cycle area spans the part of the song in which the two synths, the drums, and the bass play, so you can focus on adjusting the sounds of those instruments. Later, when you're ready to work with the piano, you will just drag the cycle area to the following four bars, where the piano plays.

7   Press the Spacebar.

Playback starts at the beginning of the cycle area, and the playhead keeps repeating bars 9 through 13, where the two synths are playing.

8   Click the Mixer button (or press X) to open the Mixer.

Synth 2 is significantly louder than Synth 1. Let's bring its level down so that both synths are equally loud.

9 In the Mixer, click the background to deselect the channel strips, and on the Synth 2 channel strip, drag down the Volume fader.

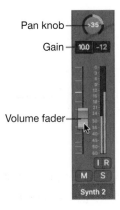

NOTE ▶ When space does not permit, negative Level and Gain values are displayed without the – (minus sign).

Continue adjusting the Volume fader until the Gain display reads 10.0. The Volume fader affects how much gain is applied to the audio signal flowing through the channel strip and, therefore, controls how loudly that instrument plays. Synth 2 is now quieter and closer to the level of Synth 1.

You will now adjust the Pan knobs on the two synth tracks to spread them farther apart in the stereo image.

10 On the Synth 1 channel strip, drag the Pan knob all the way down to –64.

11 On the Synth 2 channel strip, drag the Pan knob all the way up to +63.

The synths sound too far apart now and seem disconnected from the rhythm section. The effect is even more pronounced if you listen to the song through headphones.

Let's bring the two synths back toward the center of the mix.

12 Adjust the Synth 1 and Synth 2 pan knobs to values of about −35 and +35, respectively.

The two synths come back closer to the center of the stereo field. Now they sound like they belong in the mix.

Processing Instruments with Plug-Ins

There's more to mixing than adjusting each instrument's volume and stereo position. Now you will apply effect plug-ins to process the audio signal flowing through the channel strip, thereby changing the tone of your instruments.

In this exercise, you will use a bass amp plug-in to add an edgier character to the bass, and a reverberation plug-in to bring warmth and dimension to the piano.

1 On the Bass channel strip, click the Audio FX slot to open the plug-in menu.

2   From the menu, choose Amps and Pedals > Bass Amp Designer.

TIP When choosing a plug-in from a pop-up menu, you need to navigate to the name of the plug-in, but you don't have to select a plug-in format such as stereo or mono. When multiple formats are available in the menu, if you navigate to only the name of the plug-in, the most likely plug-in format is automatically used.

The Bass Amp Designer plug-in is inserted in the Audio FX slot on the channel strip, and its interface opens. Let's compare the sound of the bass with and without the plug-in applied.

3   Click the Power button.

The Power button dims to indicate that the plug-in is off. You can hear what the bass sounds like without the plug-in. It sounds a bit muffled and vaguely distant.

4   Click the Power button again.

The attacks of the bass notes sound brighter and have a little grit to them, giving the bass character. You could experiment with different amp models, but right now the Factory Default setting works great, so let's move on.

The bass amp also made the bass a bit louder. In fact, it is a little too loud now.

5   Close the plug-in window by clicking the close button in the upper-left corner.

6   In the Mixer, drag down the Bass Volume fader until the Gain display reads about 11.0.

You will now add a plug-in to the Piano channel strip. But first you need to move the cycle area, so you can hear the piano.

7   Stop playback.

8   In the Tracks area, in the ruler, drag the cycle area 4 bars to the right, so it goes from bar 13 to 17.

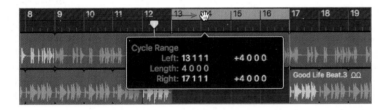

9   Start playback.

10   In the Mixer, click the Audio FX slot on the Piano channel strip.

11   From the pop-up menu, choose Reverb > Space Designer.

Let's choose a room to place the piano in.

12 At the top of the plug-in interface, from the Setting pop-up menu, choose Medium Spaces > Rooms > 1.5s Piano Warmth.

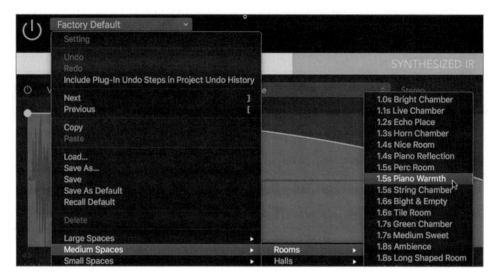

The piano immediately occupies more space and has more body. And in your arrangement, whenever the piano plays, not many other instruments are playing, so this setting works great.

13 Click the close button to close the Space Designer plug-in window.

14 Click the Mixer button (or press X) to close it.

15 In the ruler, click the cycle area (or press C) to turn off Cycle mode.

16 Play the entire song.

In the inspector, look at the peak level display on the Output channel strip. When a part of the song is too loud, the Output channel strip peak level display shows a positive value and turns red, indicating that the audio signal is distorted. In this project, the highest peak in the song is under 0 dB FS, and no distortion is created.

In a relatively short time, you have produced a one-minute instrumental song with six tracks, edited the regions in the workspace to build an arrangement, mixed the instruments in the Mixer, and added plug-ins to process their sounds. You now have a piece of music that would work fine, for example, during the credits of a radio or TV show or as a music bed for a TV ad.

Mixing Down to a Stereo File

The last step is to mix down the music to a single stereo audio file so that anyone can play it on consumer-level audio software or hardware. In this exercise, you will bounce the project to a stereo audio file. By first selecting all your regions, you avoid the need to manually adjust the bounce start and end positions.

1   In the Tracks area, choose Edit > Select > All (or press Command-A) to select all regions.

2   In the main menu bar, choose File > Bounce > Project or Section (or press Command-B) to open the Bounce dialog.

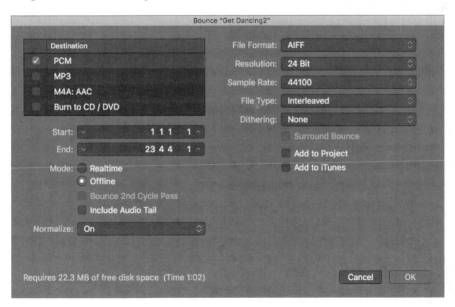

You can choose one or more Destination formats and adjust parameters for each format.

You will bounce an MP3 format file that you can easily email or upload to a website.

3   Deselect PCM and select the MP3 checkbox.

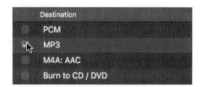

Below the Destination box, notice that the End position is correctly adjusted to the end of bar 23, when the last piano note finishes sustaining. That's because you selected all the regions in your workspace at the beginning of this exercise.

4   In the Bounce dialog, click OK (or press Return).

A Bounce dialog opens. Bouncing creates a new stereo audio file on your hard drive.

You will save the new MP3 file to your desktop.

5   In the Save As field, enter *Get Dancing Mix*, and from the Where pop-up menu, choose Desktop (or press Command-D).

6   Click Bounce (or press Return).

A Bouncing progress bar opens, and toward the end of the operation, an additional progress bar indicates the preparation of the MP3 file.

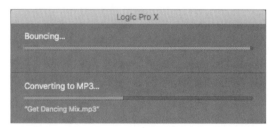

When the progress bars disappear, your MP3 file is ready on your desktop.

7   Choose Logic Pro X > Hide Logic Pro X (or press Command-H).

Logic Pro X is hidden, and you can see your desktop.

TIP ▶ If you have multiple apps open and you want to hide them all in order to see your desktop, first click the Finder icon in the Dock (or press Command-Tab to select the Finder) and choose Finder > Hide Others (or press Command-Option-H). To unhide an app, press Command-Tab to select it.

8   On your desktop, place your mouse over Get Dancing Mix.mp3, and click the play button that appears.

Your file starts playing. You can now share that MP3 file with all your friends and family!

Lesson Review

1. Where is the inspector and what are its uses?

2. Where is the Tracks area and what does it contain?

3. Where is the control bar and what does it contain?

4. Where is the workspace and what does it contain?

5. When multiple panes are open, how do you make sure the desired pane reacts to key commands?

6. Describe two ways to adjust a numerical value in Logic.

7. How do you copy a region?

8. How do you resize a region?

9. How do you loop a region?

10. In the Mixer, where do you add effect plug-ins?

11. In the help tag, what are the units of the four numeric values used to determine the length and position of a region?

12. How many ticks are there in a sixteenth note?

13. How do you mix down your project to a stereo audio file?

Answers

1. The inspector opens to the left of the Tracks area. Its contextual parameters adapt depending on which area has key focus, and what is selected.

2. The Tracks area is in the center of the main window. It contains the track headers to the left, the ruler at the top, and the workspace where you edit regions.

3. The control bar is the row of buttons and displays at the top of your display. It contains transport buttons, information LCD displays, and mode buttons.

4. The workspace is in the Tracks area, to the right of the track headers and below the ruler, and it contains the regions used in your project.

5. Click the area's background, or press the Tab key, to give it key focus.

6. Drag the value vertically, or double-click it and enter a new value.

7. Option-drag the region and always release the mouse button first, followed by the Option key.

8. Place the mouse pointer over one of the two lower corners so it changes to a Resize pointer, and then drag horizontally.

9. Select the region and press L, or select the Loop checkbox in the inspector.

10. In the Audio FX slots of the channel strips.

11. Bars, beats, divisions, and ticks

12. There are 240 ticks in a sixteenth note.

13. Choose File > Bounce > Project or Section (or press Command-B) to open the Bounce dialog.

Keyboard Shortcuts

Panels and Windows

I	Toggles the inspector
X	Toggles the Mixer
O	Opens the Loop Browser
Control-Option-Command-T	Toggles the toolbar

Navigation

Spacebar	Plays or stops project
Option-Spacebar	Preview (in windows showing audio files)
, (comma)	Rewinds one bar
. (period)	Forwards one bar
Shift-, (comma)	Rewinds eight bars
Shift-. (period)	Forwards eight bars
Return	Returns to beginning of project
U	Sets rounded locators by selection
C	Toggles Cycle mode on and off

Keyboard Shortcuts

Zooming

Control-Option-drag	Expands the dragged area to fill the workspace
Z	Expands the selection to fill workspace, or goes back to previous zoom level, and shows all regions when no regions are selected
Command-Left Arrow	Zooms out horizontally
Command-Right Arrow	Zooms in horizontally
Command-Up Arrow	Zooms out vertically
Command-Down Arrow	Zooms in vertically

General

Command-Z	Undoes the last action
Command-Shift-Z	Redoes the last action
L	Toggles Loop parameter on and off for the selected region(s)
Command-A	Selects all
Command-R	Repeats the selection once
Command-B	Bounces the project
Command-S	Saves the project
Tab	Cycles key focus forward through open panes
Shift-Tab	Cycles key focus backward through open panes

Keyboard Shortcuts

macOS

Command-D	Selects Desktop from "Where" pop-up menu in Save dialog
Command-H	Hides current application
Command-Option-H	Hides all other applications
Command-Tab	Cycles forward through open applications
Shift-Command-Tab	Cycles backward through open applications

2

Lesson Files   Logic Pro X Files > Lessons > 02 Get Dancing

Time   This lesson takes approximately 60 minutes to complete.

Goals   Choose digital audio settings

Record single and multitrack audio

Record additional takes

Record in Cycle mode

Re-record sections by punching in (manually and automatically)

Adjust count-in, metronome, and other settings

Delete unused audio files

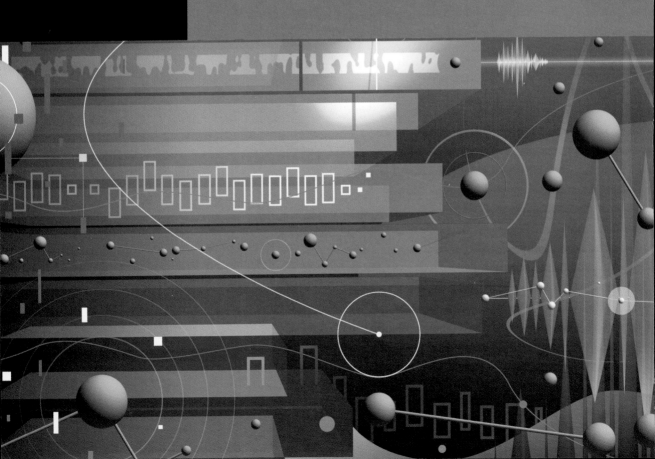

Lesson **2**

Recording Audio

To build a song, you need to come up with the raw material you will later arrange and mix. You might start with an idea you have in your head, a part you rehearsed on an instrument, or a prerecorded sample or loop, or you may just start experimenting until inspiration strikes. To sustain and develop that initial inspiration, you need to master the techniques that Logic offers to record, create, and edit the audio and MIDI regions that constitute the building blocks of your project.

In this lesson, you will configure Logic for audio recording and study activities you will typically perform when working with live musicians: recording a single instrument, recording additional takes of the same instrument, cycle recording, multitrack recording, punching on the fly, and automatic punching.

Setting Up Digital Audio Recording

Before you record audio in Logic, you must connect a sound source (such as a microphone, an electric guitar, or a synthesizer) to your Mac. You then choose the desired recording settings and adjust the recording level of your sound source to avoid distortion.

In the following exercises, you will set up Logic to prepare for a music recording.

▶ **Digital Recording, Sample Rate, and Bit Depth**

When audio is recorded in Logic Pro, sound pressure waves are turned into a digital audio file, as follows:

1. The microphone transforms sound pressure waves into an analog electrical signal.

2. The microphone preamp amplifies the analog electrical signal. A gain knob lets you set a proper recording level and avoid distortion.

3. The analog-to-digital (A/D) converter transforms the analog electrical signal into a digital data stream.

4. The audio interface sends the digital data stream from the converter to the computer.

5. Logic Pro saves the incoming data as an audio file displayed on the screen by a waveform representing the sound pressure waves.

To convert the analog signal into a digital data stream, the digital converters sample the analog signal at a very fast time interval, or *sample rate*. The sample rate identifies how many times per second the audio is digitally sampled. The *bit depth* identifies the number of data bits used to encode the value of each sample. The sample rate and bit depth settings determine the quality of a digital audio recording.

During recording, the only role for Logic is to save the digital data generated by the A/D converter to an audio file. Logic does not exert any influence over the quality of your recordings.

NOTE ▶ Most audio interfaces include analog-to-digital converters, and many include microphone preamps. Also, most modern Mac computers include a built-in audio interface. Many Mac notebook computers and iMac computers even have internal microphones. Although those microphones are generally not intended to produce professional-quality recording, you can use the internal microphones to perform the exercises in this lesson in the absence of an external microphone.

By default, Logic records with a bit depth of 24 bits, which is fine for most uses. However, you may need to use different sample rates for different projects.

Setting the Sample Rate

By setting your project's sample rate before starting your first recording, you help to ensure that all the audio files used in that project will be recorded and played at the same sample rate. Playing an audio file at the wrong sample rate will result in the wrong pitch and tempo, much like playing an audiotape or vinyl record at the wrong transport speed.

> **NOTE** ▸ Be sure to read "Installing the Logic Lesson Files" in "Getting Started" before you continue.

1   Open Logic Pro X Files > Lessons > **02 Get Dancing**.

2   Choose File > Project Settings > Audio, and make sure the General tab is selected.

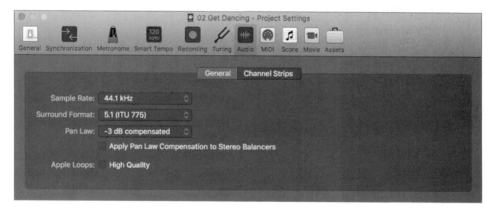

The Project Settings window opens, and you can see your Audio settings.

By default, the sample rate is set to 44.1 kHz.

To determine which sample rate to choose, consider the sample rate of any prerecorded material you will use (such as samples) and the sample rate of the target delivery medium. Some producers who make intensive use of 44.1 kHz samples choose to work at that sample rate. Traditionally, music is recorded at 44.1 kHz (which is the sample rate of compact discs), whereas audio for video is recorded at 48 kHz (which is the sample rate used on DVDs).

Note that Apple Loops (such as those used on the six existing tracks in this project) always play at the pitch and tempo determined by the project's key and tempo settings, independent of the project sample rate.

NOTE ▶ The Audio Engineering Society recommends a 48 kHz sample rate for most applications but recognizes the use of 44.1 kHz for compact disc and other consumer uses.

Let's keep the default 44.1 kHz sample rate.

3   Press Command-W to close the Project Settings window.

NOTE ▶ In Logic, settings fall into two categories: Project settings, such as the sample rate, can be set individually for each project, so that each project can have unique project settings; Logic preferences are global and apply to all projects.

Choosing an Audio Interface

In most situations, Logic automatically detects an audio interface when you connect it to your Mac and asks if you want to use that interface. If you choose to use it, Logic selects that interface as both an input and output device in its audio preferences. Let's open the audio preferences and check that the correct audio interface is selected.

1   Choose Logic Pro X > Preferences > Audio.

The Audio preferences appear.

2   From the Output Device and Input Device menus, choose the desired audio interfaces.

The Output Device is the device connected to your monitors or headphones.

The Input Device is the device into which you plug your microphones or instruments.

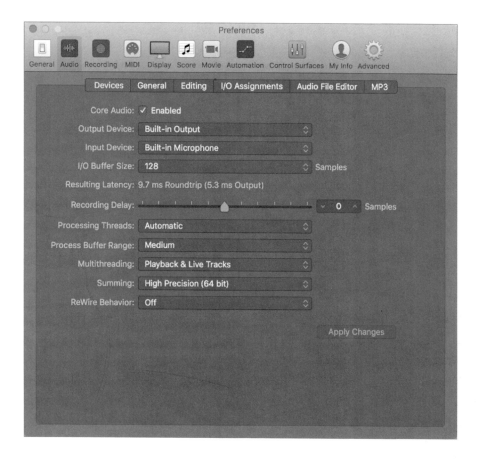

NOTE ▶ Using the same audio interface for both audio output and input is very common.

If you do not have an audio interface connected to your Mac, choose from the built-in output and input devices.

3   Press Command-W to close the Preferences window.

If you choose a new output or input device, Logic automatically reinitializes the Core Audio engine when you close the window.

MORE INFO ▶ Some options seldom need to be changed from the default settings. For more information on these, see "Changing Recording Settings" later in this lesson.

Recording a Single Track

In this example, you will record a single instrument. The exercise describes recording an electric guitar plugged directly into an instrument input on your audio interface, but feel free to record your voice or any instrument you have.

Preparing a Track for Recording

To record audio, you first have to create a new audio track, select the correct input (the input number on your audio interface where the guitar is plugged in), and enable that new track for recording.

When adding tracks, the new tracks are inserted below the selected track. To create a new track at the bottom of the Tracks area, you first need to select the bottom track.

1   At the bottom of the track headers, click the Piano track header (track 6) to select it.

2   Above the track headers, click the Add Tracks button (+) (or press Command-Option-N).

The New Tracks dialog appears.

3   Make sure the Audio track type is selected.

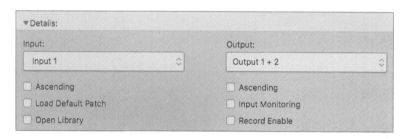

4   From the Input menu, choose the audio interface input number to which you've connected your instrument or microphone. If you are using your Mac computer's built-in
audio interface or your notebook's microphone, choose Input 1.

NOTE ▸   Below the Input and Output menus, the input and output devices selected
earlier in your Audio preferences are displayed. Should you need to change the input
and/or output device, click one of the arrow buttons to the right of the device names
to open the Audio preferences.

You can record-enable the track by selecting the Record Enable option below the Output menu; however, in some situations creating a record-enabled track may produce
feedback. You will later take precautions to avoid feedback and then record-enable the
track from the track header.

5   Ensure that "Number of tracks" is set to 1.

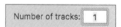

6   Click Create (or press Return).

A new audio track set to Input 1 is created. Logic automatically assigns the new track
to the next available channel. Since six audio tracks were created when you dragged
Apple Loops in Lesson 1, the new track is assigned to the Audio 7 channel and is
automatically named Audio 7. For clarity, let's rename it.

Logic automatically assigns the name of a track to the audio files recorded on that track, so naming a track before recording on it is always a good idea. If you don't name the track, Logic assigns the name of the project to the audio files. More descriptive names will help you identify files in the future.

7   In the Audio 7 track header, double-click the name, and type *Guitar.*

The new track has a generic audio waveform icon. Let's choose a more descriptive icon.

8   In the Guitar track header, Control-click the icon, and from the shortcut menu, choose the desired icon.

NOTE ▶ To avoid feedback when recording with a microphone, monitor your recording using headphones and make sure your speakers are off.

You will now set up Logic so that record-enabling a track allows you to hear the source you're recording.

9   Choose Logic Pro X > Preferences > Audio, click the General button, and make sure "Input monitoring only for focused track, and record-enabled tracks" is deselected.

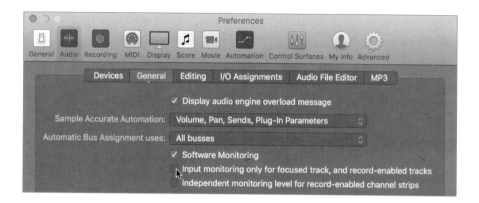

10 In the Guitar track header, click the R (Record Enable) button.

You can now hear your guitar and see its input level on the Guitar channel strip meter in the inspector.

NOTE ► You may hear a small delay between the time you play a note and when you hear it. This delay is called *latency*. You will learn how to reduce latency at the end of this lesson, in the section "Choosing the I/O Buffer Size."

Because your new audio track is record-enabled (the R button on the track header is red and blinking), the next recording will create an audio region on that track. You can monitor the audio routed to record-enabled tracks while Logic is stopped, playing, or recording.

NOTE ► If you are already using a hardware mixer or your audio interface's software to monitor the audio signal routed to record-enabled tracks, turn off Software Monitoring in Logic's audio preferences. Otherwise, you will be monitoring the signal twice, resulting in a flangy or robotic sound.

Monitoring Effects During Recording

When a guitar or bass is plugged directly into an audio interface's instrument preamp, the sound is clean and raw. To emulate the character a guitar amp can give to a guitar sound, you can use Amp Designer, a guitar amplifier modeling plug-in.

Note that you are still recording a dry guitar sound. The effect plug-in processes the dry audio signal in real time during the recording and playback. Recording a *dry signal* means that you can continue fine-tuning the effect plug-ins (or exchange them for other plug-ins) after the recording is completed.

1   In the inspector, on the Guitar channel strip, click the Audio FX insert, and choose Amps and Pedals > Amp Designer.

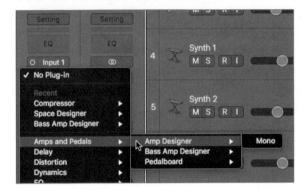

Amp Designer opens. Here, you can dial in a sound or choose a preset.

2   In the Amp Designer window, click the settings pop-up menu and choose a setting that inspires you.

You can now hear your guitar processed through Amp Designer. It sounds like a guitar plugged into a guitar amp and recorded by a microphone in front of the amp's speaker cabinet. Feel free to spend a few minutes exploring various settings and tweaking the amp's knobs until you're happy with your sound.

3   Press Command-W to close the Amp Designer window.

Adjusting the Recording Level

Before recording, make sure you can monitor the sound through Logic, and then adjust the source audio level to avoid overloading the converters. On the channel strip, look at the peak level meter, and make sure it always stays below 0 dBFS (decibels full scale, the unit used to measure levels in digital audio); a level above 0 dBFS would indicate that you are clipping the input of your converter. Keep in mind that you need to adjust the audio level before the converter input by using your microphone preamp gain knob. Allow some headroom, especially if you know that the artist might play or sing louder during the actual recording. Working with a low-level recording is better than clipping the input.

▶ **Control Your Microphone Preamp Gain Remotely Within Logic**

Compatible audio interfaces (such as a Mac computer's built-in audio device and some third-party interfaces) allow you to adjust the gain of your microphone preamp directly at the top of the audio track's channel strip in the inspector or in the Mixer. (Some interfaces also support other input settings, such as phantom power, hi-pass filter, and phase.)

▶ **Control Your Microphone Preamp Gain Remotely Within Logic** *continued*

If you cannot see the Gain knob at the top of the channel strip, Control-click the channel strip and choose Channel Strip Components > Audio Device Controls.

If the Gain knob is dimmed, it means that the feature is not supported by your audio interface.

Let's adjust the recording and monitoring levels, tune the guitar, and find a cool acoustic guitar sound.

1   Play the loudest part of the performance you are about to record, and as you watch the peak level meter on the channel strip, adjust the level on the instrument preamp.

2   If the peak level meter turns yellow or red, lower the gain on the preamp, and click the peak level meter to reset it.

Make sure the peak sits comfortably below 0 dBFS: the wider the dynamic range of the source, the more headroom it needs to avoid clipping.

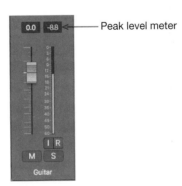

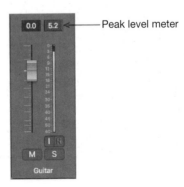

Audio not clipping   Audio clipping

When your signal peaks below –2.0 dBFS, the peak level meter value is green. When it peaks between –2.0 and 0 dBFS, the peak level meter value is yellow to indicate that you are within 2 dB of clipping (that is, you have less than 2 dB of headroom). When it peaks above 0 dBFS, the peak level meter turns red to indicate the audio is clipping.

Tuning the Instrument

Making sure an instrument is in tune before recording is always a good idea. The control bar's Tuner button gives you quick access to the Tuner plug-in.

1   In the control bar, click the Tuner button.

The Tuner opens.

NOTE ►   The Tuner is available in the control bar only when an audio track is selected and an input is selected in the input slot of the corresponding channel strip. You can also insert the Tuner as a plug-in on a channel strip: click an Audio FX slot, and choose Metering > Tuner.

2   One by one, tune the guitar strings, trying to get each string as close as possible to a 0 cents deviation of the target pitch.

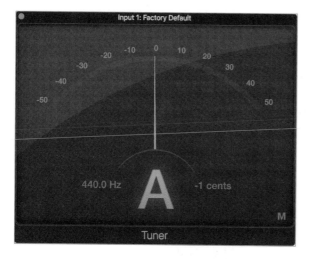

3   Close the Tuner window.

Checking the Balance

Now that the guitar is tuned, you can practice the performance and make sure that you can hear yourself and the other instruments comfortably. First, you'll turn off Auto Input Monitoring so during playback you can hear the guitar you connected.

1   Ensure that Record > Auto-Input Monitoring is deselected.

2   Press the Spacebar to start playback, and play along with the song. If the guitar is now too loud or too soft in comparison to the other tracks, in the inspector, drag the volume fader on the Guitar channel strip to adjust the monitoring level, or drag the volume slider in the Guitar track header.

The track header's volume slider and the channel strip's volume fader adjust the monitoring and playback level, but they do not alter the recording level.

3   Press the Spacebar to stop playback.

Recording Audio

You have set the desired sample rate, adjusted the recording and monitoring levels, inserted a plug-in to emulate the sound of a guitar amp, and tuned the instrument. You are now ready to start recording.

Let's record a guitar part from bar 13 to bar 17.

1   In the lower half of the ruler, click at bar 13.

The playhead is positioned at bar 13. In the control bar's LCD display, make sure the playhead position is exactly bar 13, beat 1, div 1, tick 1. If you need to adjust the position of the playhead, drag it left or right.

2   In the control bar, click the Record button (or press R).

The playhead and the LCD display in the control bar both turn red to indicate that Logic is recording. The playhead jumps one bar earlier and gives you a four-beat count-in with an audible metronome click before the recording starts. A new red region is created behind the playhead on the record-enabled track, and you can see the recording's waveform drawn in as you play or sing.

NOTE ▶ By default, the metronome automatically turns on during recording, and you get a four-beat count-in (in the control bar, the Count-in and Metronome buttons are enabled). You will learn how to alter both the metronome and the count-in settings later in this lesson.

3   After you've recorded a few bars, in the control bar, click the Stop button (or press the Spacebar).

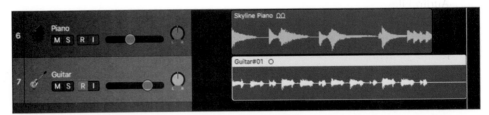

The new recording, Guitar#01, appears as a blue-shaded audio region. To the name of the track, Logic appends the number of the recording. Note that this new region is selected, which makes listening to it easy using the "Play from Selection" key command.

4   Press Shift-Spacebar.

The playhead jumps to the beginning of the selected region and playback starts.

5   Stop playback.

If you are not happy with your new recording, you can delete it and start over.

6   Press Delete.

A Delete alert appears with two choices:

▶   Delete—The audio region is removed from the Tracks area, and the audio file is removed from the Project Audio Browser. In the Finder, the audio file is moved from inside the project package to the Trash.

▶   Keep—The audio region is removed from the Tracks area. The audio file stays in the Project Audio Browser and is still present inside the project package, allowing you to later drag it back to the workspace if necessary.

NOTE ▸ To find the audio files inside a project package, Control-click the project package in the Finder, choose Show Package Contents, and then navigate to Media > Audio Files.

This alert appears only when you try to delete a recording made since you most recently opened the project. When deleting an audio region that was previously recorded, the behavior corresponding to the Keep option is automatically applied and an alert does not appear.

TIP ▸ Despite what the alert says, if you chose Delete and clicked OK by mistake, you could still choose Edit > Undo (or press Command-Z) to undo the operation (as long as you didn't empty the Trash).

You will keep your recording so you can experiment with recording additional takes in the next exercise.

7 In the Delete pop-up window, click Cancel.

Recording Additional Takes

When recording a live performance, musicians can make mistakes. Rather than deleting the previous recording and repeatedly recording until you get a flawless performance, you can record several takes (repeat performances of the same musical part) and later choose the best take, or even combine the best parts of each take to create a *comp* (composite take).

To preserve multiple takes in Logic, you can record new performances over previous ones. By default, all the takes (including the original recording) will be placed into a take folder (you can change that behavior under Record > Overlapping Audio Recordings).

1 Make sure the Guitar track is still record-enabled.

2 Position the playhead on bar 13.

3 In the control bar, click the Record button (or press R) to record a second take slightly longer than the first.

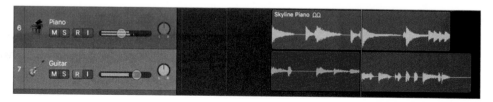

The new recording (in red) appears to be recorded over the previous blue audio region.

4   Stop the recording.

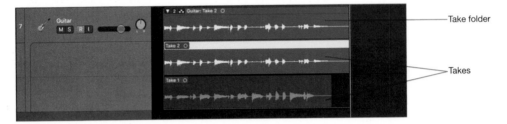

Both the original recording (Take 1) and the new recording (Take 2) have been saved into a take folder. The take folder is on the Guitar track. It is currently open, so the two takes you recorded are displayed on subtracks below.

The take folder is named Guitar: Take 2, the name of the track appended with the name of the take it's playing. By default, the take folder plays the most recent take you recorded: Take 2, in this case. The previous take, Take 1, is dimmed and muted.

NOTE ▶ If the recent take you recorded is shorter than a take you recorded earlier, the take folder is named Guitar: Comp A, and plays a comp made of the recent take and the end of the previous take.

5   Record a third take.

6   In the Guitar track header, click the R (Record Enable) button to disable it.

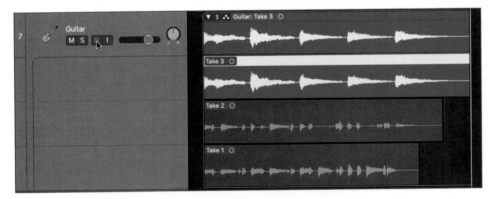

The track is disarmed, and you can no longer hear the sound coming from Input 1 on your audio interface.

The take folder now contains three takes. It plays back the most recent one, Take 3, while the two previous ones, Take 1 and Take 2, are muted.

MORE INFO ▶ You will examine take folders in more detail and learn to comp takes in Lesson 3.

7   At the top left of the Guitar take folder, click the disclosure triangle to close the folder.

TIP ▶ You can also double-click a take folder to open or close it.

Recording Takes in Cycle Mode

Recording multiple takes in a single operation can be very useful when you are both the engineer and the musician because switching from playing your instrument to operating Logic between each take isn't always practical (and it can destroy your creative vibe). Recording in Cycle mode allows you to repeatedly record a single section, thereby creating a new take for each pass of the cycle. When you stop recording, all the takes are saved inside a take folder.

1   In the upper half of the ruler, drag a cycle area from bar 5 to bar 9.

TIP ▶ You don't have to position the playhead when recording in Cycle mode; recording automatically starts at the beginning of the cycle, after the count-in.

2 Make sure the Guitar track is selected, and click Record (or press R).

The Guitar track is automatically record-enabled. The playhead jumps a bar ahead of the cycle for a one-measure count-in, and starts recording the first take. When it reaches bar 9, the end of the cycle area, it jumps back to bar 5 and starts recording a new take.

NOTE ▶ If no track is record-enabled, Logic automatically record-enables the selected track during recording.

Logic keeps looping the cycle area, recording new takes until you stop recording. Record two or three takes.

3 Click Stop (or press the Spacebar).

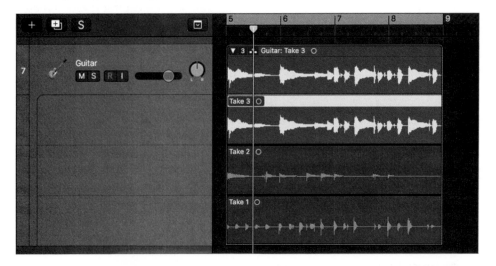

All the takes recorded in Cycle mode are packed into a take folder. The Guitar track is automatically disabled for recording.

NOTE ▶ When you stop recording, if the recent take is shorter than a bar, Logic automatically discards it. To keep the last take of a cycle recording, make sure you stop the recording more than one bar after the beginning of the cycle area.

4 At the top left of the take folder, click the disclosure triangle.

The take folder closes.

5   In the ruler, click the cycle area (or press C) to turn it off.

Recording Multiple Tracks

You can use the same single-track techniques you've learned to record multiple tracks simultaneously. Doing so allows you to record several instruments at once, placing each instrument on a separate track, so that you can later adjust their volumes and stereo positions or process them individually.

You first create the desired number of tracks, making sure that each track is assigned to a different input number that corresponds to the input number on your audio interface where the microphone is plugged in.

> **NOTE** ▸ Logic does not let you record-enable multiple tracks set to the same input number, because you would record the same input on different tracks and end up with redundant audio files.

In the following exercise, you will record two mono tracks at the same time, which you can do using the built-in Mac audio interface. To record more than two tracks at once, you need an audio interface with more than two inputs. The exercise describes recording an acoustic guitar on Input 1 and a vocal microphone on Input 2.

> **NOTE** ▸ To avoid the sound of the guitar bleeding into the vocal microphone or the sound of the vocals bleeding into the guitar microphone, the guitar player and the singer should be located in different rooms.

1   At the bottom of the Tracks area, click the Guitar track header to ensure that the tracks you are about to create will be added below the Guitar track.

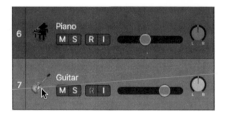

2   Above the track headers, click the Add Tracks button (+) (or press Command-Option-N) to open the New Tracks dialog.

3   At the top of the New Tracks dialog, make sure the Audio track type is selected.

4   Below the Input menu, select the Ascending checkbox.

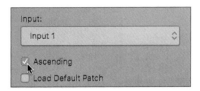

When creating multiple tracks, selecting Ascending automatically sets the inputs (or outputs) to ascending settings. In this case, you will create two tracks, so the first will be assigned to Input 1 and the second to Input 2.

Make sure that you took precautions to avoid feedback, as explained at the beginning of this lesson; this time you will create record-enabled tracks.

5   Below the Output menu, select Record Enable.

6   At the bottom of the New Tracks dialog, set "Number of tracks" to 2.

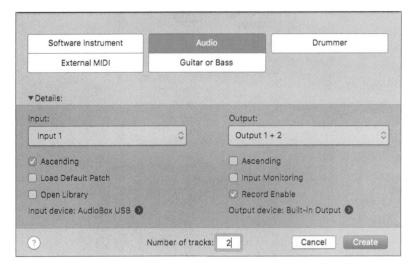

7   Click Create (or press Return).

Two new tracks are added at the bottom of the Tracks area and automatically assigned to the next available audio channels (Audio 8 and Audio 9). Their inputs are set to Input 1 and Input 2, and both are record-enabled.

TIP ▶ If you need to reassign a track's input, click the Input slot on the track's channel strip and choose the new input.

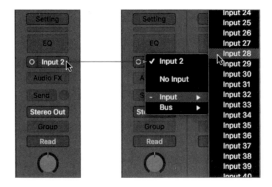

NOTE ▶ The number of inputs available in the Input menu depends on the audio interface selected as an input device in the Logic Audio preferences.

8 Rename the tracks *Acoustic Gtr* and *Vocals*.

9 In the control bar, click the Go to Beginning button (or press Return).

10 Start recording.

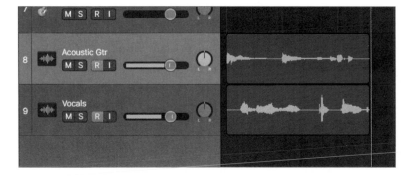

The multitrack recording starts, and after a one-measure count-in, you see the red playhead appear to the left of the workspace, creating two red regions, one on each record-enabled track.

11 After a few bars, stop recording.

You now have a new blue-shaded audio region on each track.

12 In the Acoustic Gtr and Vocals track headers, click the R (Record Enable) buttons to disable recording for both tracks.

You can use the same procedure to simultaneously record as many tracks as needed. If the tracks already exist in the Tracks area, make sure you assign them the correct inputs, record-enable them, and start recording.

NOTE ▶ You can record multiple takes on multiple tracks the same way you previously recorded to a single track: either return the playhead to the beginning of the first take and record a new take, or record multiple takes in Cycle mode.

Punching In and Out

When you want to correct a specific section of a recording—usually to fix a performance mistake—you can restart playback before the mistake, punch in to engage recording just before the section you wish to fix, and then punch out to stop recording immediately after the section while playback continues. A take folder is created, containing a comp that combines the old recording outside the punch-in/punch-out range with the new recording inside that range. This technique allows you to fix smaller mistakes in a recording while still listening to the continuity of the performance.

TIP ▶ Punching is nondestructive. At any time, you can open the take folder and select the original recording.

There are two punching methods: on the fly and automatic. Punching on the fly allows you to press a key to punch in and out while Logic plays, whereas automatic punching requires you to identify the autopunch area in the ruler before recording. Punching on the fly is fast but usually requires an engineer to perform the punch-in and punch-out while the musician is performing. Automatic punching is ideal for the musician-producer who is working alone.

Assigning Key Commands

To punch on the fly, you will use the Record Toggle command, which is unassigned by default. First, you'll open the Key Commands window and assign Record Toggle to a key combination.

1   Choose Logic Pro X > Key Commands > Edit (or press Option-K) to open the Key Commands window. Click the disclosure triangle next to Global Commands.

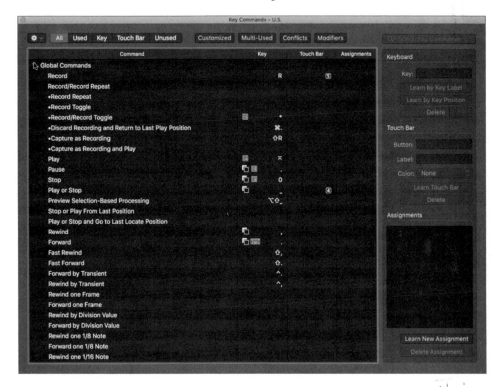

The Key Commands window lists all available Logic commands and their keyboard shortcuts, if any.

> **TIP**   Many commands are unassigned by default. When looking for a specific functionality in Logic Pro X, open the Key Commands window and try to locate the function using the search field. A command likely exists for that functionality that may or may not be assigned.

2   In the Command list, click the Record Toggle command to select it.

3   Click Learn by Key Label.

When Learn by Key Label is selected, you can press a key, or a key plus a combination of modifiers (Command, Control, Shift, Option), to create a keyboard command for the selected function.

4   Press R.

An alert indicates that the R key is already assigned to the Record command. You could click Replace to assign R to Record Toggle, but then Record would no longer be assigned to a keyboard shortcut. Instead, let's use another key combination.

5   Click Cancel (or press Esc).

6   Press Control-J.

Control-J is now listed in the Key column next to Record Toggle, indicating that the command was successfully assigned.

TIP ▶ To unassign a key command, select the command, make sure Learn by Key Label is selected, and press Delete.

7   Close the Key Commands window.

TIP ▶ To reset all key commands to their defaults, choose Logic Pro X > Key Commands > Presets > U.S. (or the language of your choice).

Punching on the Fly

You will now use the Record Toggle key command you assigned in the previous exercise to punch on the Vocals track (the bottom track in your Tracks area).

1   In the Vocals track header, click the R button to record-enable the track.

When punching on the fly, you may first want to play the performance to determine which section needs to be re-recorded, and to be ready to punch in and out at the desired locations.

2   Listen to the Vocals track and determine where you're going to punch in and out.

3   In the control bar, click the Go to Beginning button (or press Return).

4   Click Play (or press the Spacebar) to start playback.

Position your fingers on the keyboard to be ready to press your Record Toggle key command when you reach the point where you want to punch in.

NOTE ▶ To be able to punch on the fly, make sure Record > Allow Quick Punch-In is selected.

5   Press Control-J (Record Toggle).

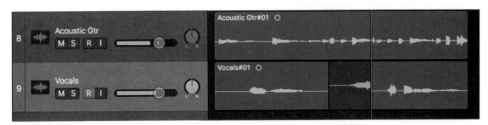

The playhead continues moving, but Logic is now recording a new take on top of the previous recording. Keep your fingers in position to be ready to punch out.

6   Press Control-J again.

The recording stops while the playhead continues playing the project.

7   Stop the playback.

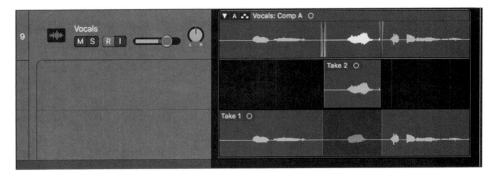

On the Vocals track, a take folder was created. It contains your original recording (Take 1) and the new take (Take 2). A comp is automatically created (Comp A) that combines the original recording up to the punch-in point, the new take between the punch-in and punch-out points, and the original recording after the punch-out point. Fades are automatically applied at the punch-in and punch-out points. (You will learn more about fades in Lesson 3.)

8   Listen to your Vocals track.

In the next exercise, you will examine another punching technique, so let's undo this recording.

9   Choose Edit > Undo Recording (or press Command-Z).

The take folder disappears, and you once again see the Vocals#01 region on the
Vocals track.

Punching on the fly is a great technique that allows the musician to focus on his performance while the engineer takes care of punching in and out at the right times. On the
other hand, if you worked alone through this exercise and tried to punch in and punch
out while playing your instrument or singing, you realize how challenging it can be. When
working alone, punching automatically is recommended.

Punching Automatically

To prepare for automatic punching, you enable the Autopunch mode and set the autopunch area. Setting the punch-in and punch-out points in advance allows you to focus
entirely on your performance during recording.

First, you will customize the control bar to add the Autopunch button.

1   Control-click the control bar, and choose Customize Control Bar and Display.

A dialog opens in which you can choose the buttons you would like to see in the control bar, and the information you'd like to see in its LCD display.

2   In the dialog's Modes and Functions column, select Autopunch to add the Autopunch
button to the control bar.

NOTE ▶ The control bar is customized independently for each Logic project file,
which allows you to show different buttons and displays, depending on the specific
needs of each project.

3 Click the Autopunch button (or press Command-Control-Option-P).

NOTE ▶ When the main window is not wide enough for the control bar to display all the buttons selected in the control bar customization dialog, you can click the chevron (>>) to the right of the mode buttons to access the hidden functions in a shortcut menu.

The ruler becomes taller to accommodate for the red autopunch area.

The autopunch area defines the section to be re-recorded. You can define the autopunch area with more precision when you can clearly see where the mistakes are on the audio waveform.

TIP ▶ Option-Command-click the ruler to toggle the Autopunch mode.

4 Click the background of the workspace to deselect every region.

5 On the Vocals track, click the Vocals#01 region to select it.

6 Press Z.

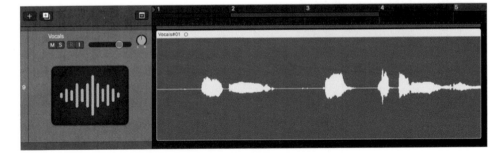

Logic zooms in, and the selected region fills the workspace.

7 Listen to the vocal recording and determine which section you're going to fix.

Here we have a vocal recording in which the two words around bar 3 need to be re-recorded. Listen while watching the playhead move over the waveform to determine which part of the waveform corresponds to the words you need to replace.

8 Adjust the autopunch area so that it encompasses the area you want to re-record.

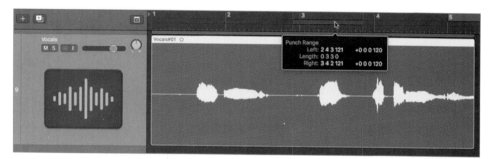

You can drag the edges of the autopunch area to resize it, or drag the entire area to move it. Red vertical guidelines help you align the punch-in and punch-out points with the waveform. Feel free to zoom in closer to make sure you're re-recording exactly what you want.

9 Click Go to Beginning (or press Return).

10 Click Record (or press R).

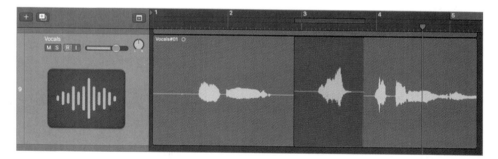

Playback starts. In the control bar, the Record button blinks; Logic isn't yet recording.

When the playhead reaches the punch-in point (the left edge of the autopunch area), the Record button turns solid red and Logic starts recording a new take.

When the playhead reaches the punch-out point (the right edge of the autopunch area), the recording stops but the playback continues.

11 Stop playback.

A take folder, Vocals: Comp A, is created on the track.

12 Click the name of the take folder to select it.

13 Press Z.

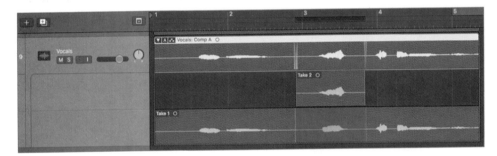

Logic zooms out so you can see the entire take folder filling the workspace.

Just as when you punched on the fly in the previous exercise, a comp is automatically created that plays the original recording up to the punch-in point, inserts the new take between the punch-in and punch-out points, and continues with the original recording after the punch-out point.

14 In the control bar, click the Autopunch button (or press Command-Control-Option-P) to disable Autopunch mode.

15 At the top left of the take folder, click the disclosure triangle to close the take folder.

16 Save your work and close the project.

TIP ▶ You can speed up the Autopunch recording process by using the Marquee tool described in Lesson 3. When a marquee selection is present, starting a recording automatically turns on the Autopunch mode, and the autopunch area matches the marquee selection.

Recording Without a Metronome

Musicians often use a tempo reference when recording. In most modern music genres, when live drums are used, drummers record their performance while listening to a metronome or a click track. When electronic drums are used, they are often recorded or programmed first, and then quantized to a grid so that they follow a constant tempo. The other musicians later record their parts while listening to this drum track.

Still, some musicians prefer to play to their own beat and record their instrumental tracks without following a metronome, click track, or drum track. When recording audio in Logic, you can set up Smart Tempo to analyze a recording and automatically create a tempo map that follows the performance so that the notes end up on the correct bars and beats. Subsequent recording or MIDI programming can then follow that tempo map, ensuring that all tracks play in sync.

1   Choose File > New.

An empty project template opens, and the New Tracks dialog opens.

2   In the New Tracks dialog, ensure that Audio is selected, and click Create.

To make Logic analyze the audio recording and create a corresponding tempo map, you should set the Project Tempo mode to Adapt.

3   Below the tempo value, click the Project Tempo mode, and choose "ADAPT – Adapt Project Tempo."

The Global Tempo track opens, and the tempo curve is shaded in orange. The orange color indicates that those parameters will be affected by a new recording.

Get ready to record. You can sing or play any instrument you'd like as long as your performance has a clearly audible rhythm.

4   Click Record, or press R.

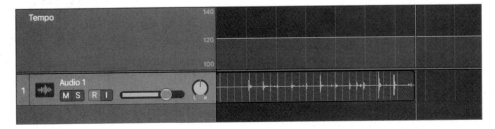

Because the Project Tempo mode is set to Adapt, the metronome does not automatically play (unlike the Project Tempo mode set to Keep mode). You no longer need it!

Because you have no time reference, you needn't rush. You can choose to start performing whenever you're ready. Try playing something that has an obvious rhythmic quality to it, such as a staccato rhythm part in which you can clearly distinguish the individual chords or notes.

During the recording, Logic displays red vertical lines over the recording when it detects beats.

5   Click Stop, or press the Spacebar.

An alert offers to open the File Tempo Editor so you can preview the recording and adjust the positions of the beat markers that Logic created while analyzing the file.

6   Click Don't Show.

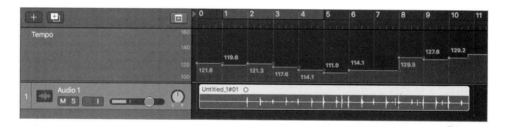

In the Global Tempo track, you can see multiple tempo changes. This new tempo map reflects the tempo at which you played during the recording, and unless you're a human metronome, chances are good that the tempo fluctuates from bar to bar, and sometimes even from beat to beat. Let's see how close Logic got to detecting the tempo of your performance.

7   Click the Metronome button, or press K.

8   Listen to your recording.

If you're lucky, the metronome follows the tempo of the performance, and sounds in sync with your recording. If you're unlucky, Logic got it wrong and the result can be messy. In that case, perform this exercise again, making sure you can hear a strong rhythmic reference in your recording. (For example, try tapping a very basic beat with your fingers in front of the microphone.)

9 Close the project without saving it.

You have recorded a rubato performance without listening to a timing reference. Logic automatically detected your tempo changes and applied them to the project tempo. You've only just begun to scratch the surface of what you can do with Smart Tempo, which you will explore further in Lesson 7.

Changing Recording Settings

Although you can immediately record audio with Logic Pro X, sometimes you'll want to change its default recording settings. Some settings do not affect the quality of the audio recording but can alter the behavior of your project during recording or change the audio file format used for recordings. The next few exercises will show you how those settings affect the audio recording process and explain how to modify them.

Setting the Count-In

The count-in is the time you have to prepare yourself and get in the groove before the actual recording begins.

1 Open Logic Pro X Files > Lessons > 02 Get Dancing.

2 On the Vocals track at the bottom of the workspace, click the take folder to select it, and press Delete.

The take folder is deleted.

3 Go to the beginning of the project.

Until now, every time you pressed Record, the playhead jumped to the beginning of the previous measure so you could have a four-beat count-in. However, sometimes you may want to start recording without a count-in.

4 In the control bar, click the Count-in button to turn off count-in.

5 Start recording, and stop after a couple of bars.

The playhead starts from its current position, and Logic starts recording right away.

At other times, you may need a longer count-in, or you may want Logic to count in for a specific number of beats.

6 Press Command-Z to undo the recording.

The audio region is removed from the workspace, but the audio file is still in the project folder.

See the "Deleting Unused Audio Files" section later in this lesson to learn how to delete all unused recordings by using the Project Audio Browser.

7 From the main menu, choose Record > Count-in > 2 Bars.

8 Position the playhead at bar 5, and start recording.

The playhead jumps two bars ahead to bar 3, and playback starts. When the playhead reaches bar 5, Logic starts recording.

NOTE ▶ When selecting a count-in between one bar and six bars, playback always starts at the beginning of a bar, even when you start recording in the middle of a bar.

9 Stop recording and press Command-Z to undo the recording.

Let's reset the count-in to its original value.

10 From the main menu, choose Record > Count-in > 1 Bar.

Setting the Metronome

By default, the metronome is turned off during playback and automatically plays during recording. In this exercise, you will change the default behaviors using the Metronome button and later go into the Metronome settings to adjust its sounds.

1   In the control bar, click the Metronome button to turn it on.

2   Start playback.

The metronome is on.

3   Stop playback and start recording.

The metronome is on.

4   While Logic is still recording, turn off the metronome.

The metronome is off.

5   Stop recording.

The metronome is back on. You now have inverted the default behavior: the metronome is on during playback and is automatically turned off during recording.

6   In the control bar, Control-click the Metronome button, and deselect Click While Playing.

The metronome is now off regardless of whether you're playing or recording.

7   Control-click the Metronome button, and choose Metronome Settings.

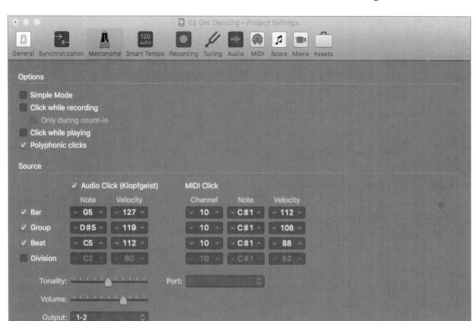

The Metronome Settings window opens. There are settings for two metronomes: Audio Click (also known as Klopfgeist, which is German for *knocking ghost*), which you are using, and MIDI Click, which is now off.

NOTE ▶ If you want your metronome to play a specific sound on an external hardware MIDI synthesizer, sampler, or drum machine, use the MIDI Click. From the Port menu, choose a MIDI Out port, and connect a MIDI cable from that MIDI Out port on the MIDI Interface to the MIDI In port on your hardware sampler/synthesizer.

Under the name of each metronome, you can adjust the pitch and velocity of the notes playing on each bar and beat. You can play a sound on every division, which can be useful when you're working with very slow tempos.

8   In the Metronome settings window, select "Click while playing."

9   Go to the beginning of the song and start playback.

The metronome sounds a little low compared to the drum loop on track 1. In fact, you can hear it only when no drum hit occurs on that beat. At the bottom of the Metronome Settings window, you can drag a couple of sliders to adjust the sound of the metronome.

10 Drag the Volume slider all the way to the right.

Even with the volume turned all the way up, it's challenging for a dry metronome sound to cut through a busy mix, and you still have to strain to hear it, especially starting at bar 5, where the bass and drums come in.

11 Drag the Tonality slider slowly toward the right.

The metronome sound changes, and you can start hearing a pitch. Adjusting the tonality of the metronome is important: a pitched sound (slider to the right) will better cut through a busy mix, but it will also bleed through the musician's headphones into the microphone. A more muted sound (slider to the left) is more suitable for quiet mixes in which you can't tolerate any metronome bleed.

12 Adjust the metronome so that it is loud and clear.

When a project already contains a drum track, you may need the metronome only during the count-in to get into the groove before the song starts.

13 At the top of the Metronome Settings window, under Options, select "Click while recording" and "Only during count-in."

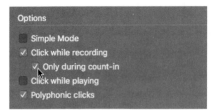

14 Close the Settings window, go to the beginning of the project, and start recording.

You hear the metronome for one measure, and then it stops playing as the song and the recording start at bar 1.

15 Stop and undo the recording.

16 Click the Metronome button to turn it off.

Choosing the I/O Buffer Size

When communicating with the audio interface, Logic does not receive or transmit just one sample at a time. It places a number of samples in an input buffer for recording and in an output buffer for monitoring. When a buffer is full, Logic processes or transmits the entire buffer. The larger the buffers, the less computing power is required from the CPU. The advantage of using larger input and output buffers is that the CPU has more time to calculate other processes, such as instrument and effects plug-ins. The drawback to using a larger buffer is that you may have to wait a bit for the buffer to fill before you can monitor your signal. That means a longer delay between the original sound and the one you hear through Logic, a delay called *roundtrip latency*.

Usually, you want the shortest possible latency when recording and the most available CPU processing power when mixing so that you can use more plug-ins. You can adjust the I/O buffer size depending on your situation.

1 Choose Logic Pro X > Preferences > Audio.

The Audio preferences pane opens. The default I/O Buffer Size is 128 Samples, which should have a latency of about 10 to 20 ms (milliseconds) for most devices.

NOTE ▶ The driver used by your audio interface also influences the roundtrip latency. Depending on the audio device selected in your Audio preferences, you may see different latencies for the same I/O buffer size. When choosing a different audio device, make sure you click Apply Changes to update the Resulting Latency value displayed.

2   From the I/O Buffer Size pop-up menu, choose 32.

The latency is now shorter.

NOTE ▶ Acoustic sound waves travel through air at roughly one foot per millisecond, so a guitar player whose ear is five feet from her guitar amp's speaker will hear notes approximately five milliseconds after playing them.

3   Close the Preferences window.

The Core Audio engine is initialized with a 32-samples I/O buffer.

To monitor the impact of the I/O buffer size on the CPU, you need to customize the control bar to display the CPU meter.

4   In the control bar, click the small arrow to the right of the LCD display, and choose Custom.

The LCD display now displays more information, including CPU and HD meters to the right.

5   Double-click the CPU or HD meter.

The CPU/HD window appears with more detailed meters. If your Mac has a multi-core CPU, you can see a meter for each core.

6   Start playback at bar 13.

To avoid putting too much stress on your CPU, let's reset the I/O buffer to its default size.

7   Choose Logic Pro X > Preferences > Audio.

8   Set the I/O buffer size to 128.

9   Close the Preferences window.

NOTE ▸ Depending on your Mac computer's CPU, you may not see the same number of cores or the same amount of activity on the meters.

You can monitor the amount of work each core is doing. When the CPU works harder, you might hear pops and crackles while the song plays. When playing the project becomes too much work for the CPU, playback stops and you will see an error alert.

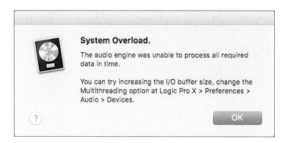

When that happens, you can try raising the I/O buffer size and reinitializing the audio engine. However, if you try to record audio with a high I/O buffer size, you will hear a delay between the notes you play and the notes you hear. That's latency. If you intend to do more audio recordings, find the lowest I/O buffer size setting that still allows clean monitoring.

NOTE ▶ Some audio effect plug-ins can also introduce latency. Choose Record > Low Latency Mode to automatically bypass those plug-ins.

Deleting Unused Audio Files

The Project Audio Browser shows all the audio files and audio regions that have been imported or recorded in your project. During a recording session, the focus is on capturing the best possible performance, and you may want to avoid burdening yourself with the decision making that comes with deleting bad takes. You may also have several unused audio files in the Project Audio Browser that make the project package (or folder) bigger than it needs to be.

In this next exercise, you will select and delete all unused audio files from your hard drive.

1   In the control bar, click the Browsers button (or press F) and ensure that the Project tab is selected.

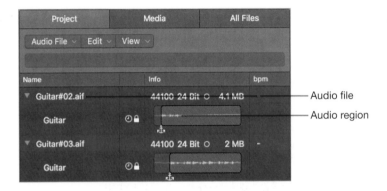

The Project Audio Browser opens, listing all the Apple Loops used on tracks 1 through 6, and all the audio files you've recorded during this lesson.

For each audio file, the Info column shows:

▶ Sample rate (44,100 Hz)

▶ Bit depth (24 bits)

▶ Format icon (a single circle indicates a mono audio file)

▶ File size

Clicking the disclosure triangle in front of the audio filename toggles the display of audio regions referring to that audio file.

NOTE ▶ Resizing, cutting, or copying regions in the workspace is called nondestructive editing. The audio data in the audio file stays intact, and the regions merely point to different sections of the audio file. You will learn more about nondestructive editing in Lesson 3.

2   In the workspace, select any audio regions you don't want to keep, and then press Delete. If a Delete alert appears, select Keep and click OK.

The regions are removed from the workspace, but their parent audio files are still present in the Project Audio Browser.

3   From the Project Audio Browser menu, choose Edit > Select Unused (or press Shift-U).

All the audio files that do not have an associated region in the workspace are selected.

NOTE ▶ If you're not sure about deleting the files, preview a region by selecting it and clicking the Prelisten button (or press Option-Spacebar). While the region plays, a small white playhead travels through the regions.

TIP ▶ In the Project Audio Browser, to play a region from a specific point, click and hold down the mouse button over its waveform at the desired location.

Once you feel satisfied that the selected audio files do not contain any useful material, you can delete them.

4   From the Project Audio Browser menu bar, choose Audio File > Delete File(s).

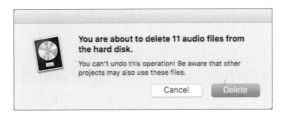

An alert asks you to confirm the deletion.

5   Click Delete.

The audio files are removed from the Project Audio Browser. In the Finder, the files are moved to the Trash.

You are now ready to tackle many recording situations: you can record a single track or multiple tracks, add new takes in a take folder, and fix mistakes by punching on the fly or automatically. You know where to adjust the sample rate, and you understand which settings affect the behavior of the software during a recording session. And you can reduce the file size of your projects by deleting unused audio files—which will save disk space, and download and upload time should you wish to collaborate with other Logic users over the Internet.

Lesson Review

1. What two fundamental settings affect the quality of a digital audio recording?
2. In Logic, where can you find the sample rate setting?
3. What precaution must you take before record-enabling multiple tracks simultaneously?
4. In Autopunch mode, how do you set the punch-in and punch-out points?
5. Describe an easy way to access your Metronome settings.
6. Describe an easy way to access your count-in settings.
7. What happens when you raise the I/O buffer size?
8. In the Project Audio Browser, when selecting unused files, what determines whether a file is used or unused?

Answers

1. The sample rate and the bit depth

2. The sample rate is found under File > Project Settings > Audio.

3. Make sure the tracks are assigned different inputs.

4. Adjust the left and right edge of the autopunch area in the middle of the ruler.

5. Control-click the Metronome button, and choose Metronome settings.

6. In the main menu, choose Record > Count-in, and choose the appropriate setting.

7. The CPU works less hard so you can use more plug-ins, but the roundtrip latency is longer.

8. An audio file is considered unused when no regions present in the workspace refer to that file.

Keyboard Shortcuts

Recording

R	Starts recording
Command-Control-Option-P	Toggles Autopunch mode
Option-Command-click the ruler	Toggles Autopunch mode

Tracks

Command-Option-N	Opens New Tracks dialog

Key Commands

Option-K	Opens Key Commands window

Project Audio Browser

F	Opens or closes the Browser pane
Shift-U	Selects unused audio files

3

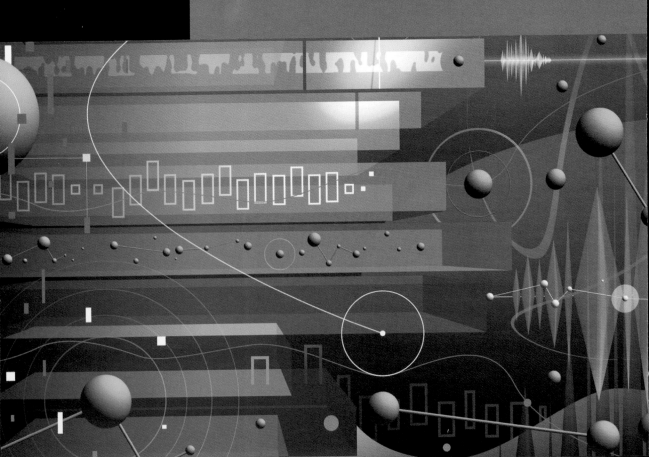

Lesson 3
Editing Audio

Audio engineers have always looked for new ways to edit recordings. In the days of magnetic recording, they used razor blades to cut pieces of a recording tape and then connected those pieces with special adhesive tape. They could create a smooth transition (or crossfade) between two pieces of magnetic tape by cutting at an angle.

Digital audio workstations revolutionized audio editing. The waveform displayed on the screen is a visual representation of the digital audio recordings stored on the hard disk. The ability to read that waveform and manipulate it using the Logic editing tools is the key to precise and flexible audio editing.

In this lesson, you will edit audio regions nondestructively in the workspace and the Audio Track Editor, and add fades and crossfades. You will open a take folder and use Quick Swipe Comping to create a single composite take. Finally, you'll reverse a guitar recording to create a swelling sound effect, and use the Flex tool to correct the timing of a guitar recording.

Even as your ability to read waveforms and use the Logic editing tools develops, never forget to use your ears and trust them as the final judge of your work.

Assigning Mouse Tools

Until now, you have exclusively worked with the default tools. You have also used keyboard modifiers such as Control-Option to choose the Zoom tool, and changed the pointer to tools such as the Resize or Loop tools. When editing audio in the workspace, you will need to access even more tools.

In the Tracks area (and in various editors), two menus are available to assign the Left-click tool and the Command-click tool.

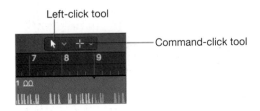

Left-click tool

Command-click tool

Previewing and Naming Regions

During recording sessions, helping the talent produce the best possible performance often takes priority over secondary tasks such as naming regions. In the aftermath of such sessions, when you don't know what musical material is contained in the regions on a track, taking the time to preview those tracks and give them descriptive names will help prepare for an efficient editing session.

In this exercise, you will assign tools to the mouse pointer. You will use the Solo tool to preview the audio regions on the new Guitar track, and apply the Text tool to rename them.

1   Open Logic Pro X Files > Lessons > **03 Get Dancing**.

2   In the Tracks area menu bar, click the Left-click Tool menu, and choose the Solo tool.

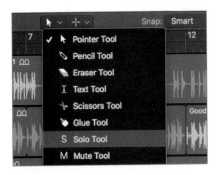

When placed over a region, the mouse pointer has a little S next to it, indicating that it's a Solo tool. You can hear a region play back in solo mode by placing the Solo tool over the region and holding down the mouse button.

Let's first make sure the scrubbing preference is turned on.

3   Choose Logic Pro X > Preferences > Audio. Click the Editing tab and make sure "Scrubbing with audio in Tracks area" is selected.

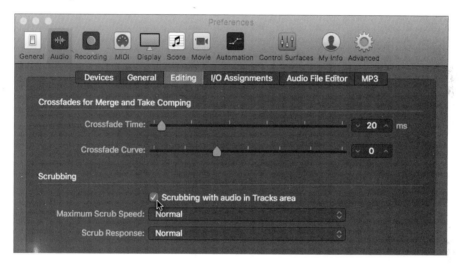

4   With the Solo tool over the Guitar track (track 7), hold down the mouse button at the beginning of the *Guitar #10.4* region.

In the control bar, the Solo button turns on, and the LCD display and the playhead both turn yellow. The region is soloed, and you can play back starting from the location where you placed the Solo tool.

You can also drag the Solo tool to scrub the region. You can change the playback speed or direction by dragging the Solo tool to the right or to the left. This technique can be useful when you're trying to locate a specific piece of audio material within a region.

You can hear that the guitar is playing single, muted notes, so you will give it a descriptive name based on those notes.

5 Click the Command-click Tool menu, and choose the Text tool.

Your Left-click Tool menu now displays the Solo tool, and the Command-click Tool menu displays the Text tool. If you hold down Command when your pointer is over a region, it changes to the Text tool.

6 Command-click the *Guitar#10.4* region.

A text field appears, in which you can enter a new name for the region.

7 Type *Muted Single Notes*, and press Return to rename that region.

8 Farther to the right on the same Guitar track, using the Solo tool, hold down the mouse button in the Guitar take folder at bar 13.

You can hear some dead notes at the beginning of this take folder, and about a bar of funk rhythm guitar (in bar 14). You will edit this take folder later in this lesson.

9 Command-click the take folder, and rename it *Funk Rhythm*.

10 Using the Solo tool, listen to each one of the three small regions at the end of the Guitar track.

> **TIP** ▸ To make sure you start playback from the beginning of each region, Option-click the region with the Solo tool.

In those regions, the guitar sustains chords, so you will name the regions after the chord names. When naming multiple regions, you may find it cumbersome to repeatedly hold down Command, so let's assign the Text tool to the Left-click tool.

Instead of moving back and forth from the workspace to the tool menus in the Tracks area menu bar, you can press T to open the Tool menu at the current pointer position.

11 Press T (Show Tool Menu).

A Tool menu appears at the pointer position. This key command will save you a lot of trips to the title bar.

NOTE ► Different areas of the main window (such as the Tracks area or the editors) have their own sets of tools. You can change an area's tools in the Tool menus in its menu bar, or by positioning the pointer over that area and pressing T.

12 In the Tool menu, choose the Text tool.

TIP ► When the Tool menu is open, you can press the key command listed to the right of a tool to assign that tool to the Left-click tool.

13 Rename the last three regions on the Guitar track: *Ab chord, Bb chord*, and *Cm chord*.

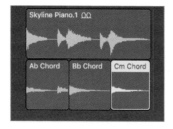

You can also Command-click a tool in the pop-up Tool menu to assign it to the Command-click tool.

14 Press T to reopen the Tool menu, and Command-click the Marquee tool.

Now, let's return the Left-click tool to the Pointer tool.

15 Press T twice.

The Tool menu opens and closes, and the Left-click tool reverts to the Pointer tool.

Both tools are back to their default assignments: the Pointer tool for the Left-click tool and the Marquee tool for the Command-click tool.

TIP ▶ If you have a two-button mouse, you can assign a third tool to the right mouse button by choosing Logic Pro X > Preferences > General and clicking the Editing tab. From the Right Mouse Button pop-up menu, choose "Is Assignable to a Tool." The Right-click Tool menu will appear to the right of the two existing Tool menus.

Now that you know how to choose the best tool for the job, you're ready to start editing the audio regions on the Guitar track.

Editing Regions in the Workspace

Editing audio regions in the workspace is nondestructive. Regions are merely pointers that identify parts of an audio file. When you cut and resize regions in the workspace, only those pointers are altered. No processing is applied to the original audio files, which remain untouched on your hard disk. As a result, editing in the workspace provides a lot of flexibility and room for experimentation because you can always adjust your edits at a later date.

In this next exercise, you will edit the *Muted Single Notes* region on the Guitar track. You will first resize the region to make it exactly four measures long, and then you'll use the Marquee tool to select some of the audio material in the region and copy it later in the track.

Since you'll be working with whole bars, you'll first choose snap modes to make the mouse pointer snap to bar lines on the grid, making the editing session easier and faster.

1   At the top of the Tracks area, from the Snap menu, choose Bar.

NOTE ▶ If the Tracks area is not wide enough to display the Snap menu in its menu bar, click the action pop-up menu that appears and choose Snap > Bar.

In the Snap menu, a checkmark appears in front of the modes you choose.

2   From the Snap menu, choose Snap Regions to Absolute Value.

3   On the Guitar track (track 7), on the *Muted Single Notes* region, drag the Resize tool toward the left until the region end snaps to bar 9.

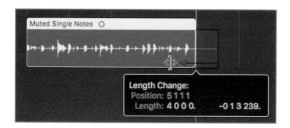

The help tag shows that the region length is now 4 0 0 0.

TIP ▶ To disable snapping when using various tools in the workspace, hold down the mouse button to start using the tool, and then hold down Control or (for even greater precision) Control-Shift.

4   Listen from the beginning of the song to the end of the *Muted Single Notes* region.

You will now repeat the simple motif in the last two bars of the *Muted Single Notes* region a couple more times, from bars 9 to 13, where the synthesizers play.

The Command-click tool is now the Marquee tool, and the Left-click tool is the Pointer tool. This is a very powerful tool combination when editing audio in the workspace. You can select a section of an audio region with the Marquee tool, and move or copy that selection using the Pointer tool.

5   Command-drag the waveform in the *Muted Single Notes* region from bar 7 to bar 9.

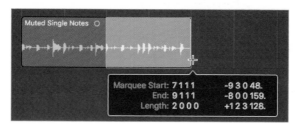

The section you selected with the Marquee tool is highlighted.

6   Press the Spacebar to play the selection.

TIP ▶ When a marquee selection is present, playback starts at the beginning and stops at the end of that marquee selection, even when Cycle mode is turned on.

The playhead jumps to bar 7 and plays the selection. It corresponds exactly to the two-bar pattern of the guitar you are going to copy.

7   Option-drag the marquee selection to bar 9, first releasing the mouse button and then releasing the Option key.

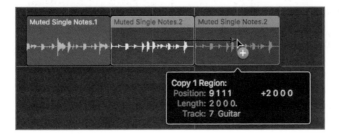

Option-dragging a marquee selection automatically divides, copies, and pastes the selection to a new location regardless of region boundaries. In this example, the two-bar guitar pattern is copied and pasted at bar 9.

Remember to release the mouse button first and the Option key second. When the mouse button is released, the original region is automatically restored.

8   Option-drag the new two-bar *Muted Single Notes.3* region to bar 11.

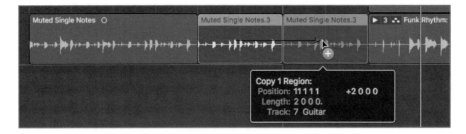

9   Listen from the beginning of the song to the Funk Rhythm take folder at bar 13.

The guitar plays a melodic riff with high notes when it first comes in, and then it plays more discretely throughout the following sections, leaving room for the two synths to shine.

Still, you can bring back a little bit of the excitement just before the breakdown at bar 13.

10 In the first *Muted Single Notes* region, Command-drag from bar 6 to bar 7.

11 Option-drag the marquee selection to bar 12.

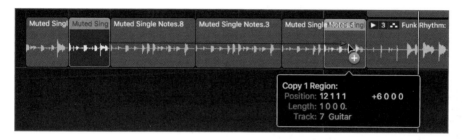

In the Tracks area menu bar, the Drag pop-up menu shows the default drag mode, "No Overlap." As you copy the new region to bar 12, the two-bar region that existed at bar 11 is trimmed down to a one-bar region to make space for the new region.

12 Click the background to clear the Marquee selection.

13 Listen to this new edit.

This last region brings back a welcome variation to the monotonous pattern that the guitar has been playing for the past five bars, returning in time to lead to the break in the next section.

Now you know how to select the desired material within a region and move or copy that material anywhere on the track. You could, for example, move or copy a single drum hit, or a single word in a vocal performance, to replace another one that doesn't sound as good.

Comping Takes

In the previous lesson, you recorded several takes of a guitar performance and packed them into a take folder. Now you will learn how to preview those individual takes and assemble a composite take by choosing sections from multiple takes, a process called *comping*.

Comping techniques are useful when you have recorded several takes of the same musical phrase, each with its good and bad qualities. In the first take, the musician may have messed up the beginning but played the ending perfectly. And in the following take, he nailed the beginning and made a mistake at the end. You can create a perfectly played comp using the beginning of the second take and the ending of the first take.

You can use the same comping techniques to create a single musical passage from multiple musical ideas. As they improvise in the studio, musicians will often record a few takes and later comp the best ideas of each performance into a new, virtual performance.

Previewing the Takes

Before you start comping, you need to become familiar with the takes you are going to comp. While doing so, you will assign the takes different colors to help distinguish between them, and then decide which part of which take you will use.

1   At bar 13 on the Guitar track, double-click the take folder to open it.

2   Press Z to zoom in on the selection.

The selected take folder and its takes fill the workspace. The take folder is on the Guitar track, and the three takes it contains are on lanes below the Guitar track. Take 3 at the top is selected and is the take currently playing. The other takes are dimmed to indicate that they are muted.

Take Folder pop-up menu
Quick Swipe Comping button

You'll see three buttons at the upper left of a take folder:

▶   The disclosure button allows you to open or close the take folder.

▶   The Take Folder pop-up menu displays the current take number (or the current comp letter) and contains options to manage your takes and comps.

▶   The Quick Swipe Comping button allows you to toggle Quick Swipe Comping on and off to edit the individual takes in the same way you would edit regions on a track.

After those three buttons, you'll see the name you previously gave your take folder (Funk Rhythm) followed by the comp name (Take 3).

Let's assign each take a unique color.

3   Press Option-C to open the Color palette.

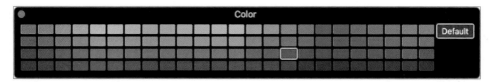

TIP ▶ The Color palette displays a white frame around the color(s) of the selected region(s). This is useful when you need to assign other regions the same color.

4   Click Take 1 to select it.

5   In the Color palette, click a purple color square.

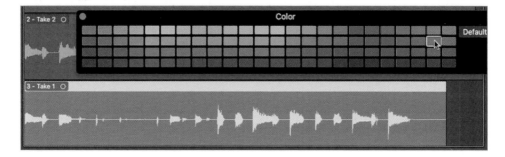

Take 1 is purple.

You will keep the blue color for Take 2, and choose a new color for Take 3.

6   Click Take 3, and in the Color palette, click a green square.

7   Close the Color palette.

8   Press Command-U to turn on Cycle mode and make the locators match the selected take.

9   In the Guitar track header, click the S (Solo) button, or make sure the Guitar track is selected and press S.

10 Press the Spacebar.

The selected take, Take 3, plays. There's really only one usable bar in this whole take—the second bar (between bars 14 and 15).

11 Stop playback, select Take 2 and listen to it.

This time the first bar sounds good, but the second bar is rather messy; the third bar sounds good, and then the guitar player plays the wrong chord and stops. So far, between Take 2 and Take 3, you have just enough material to cover the first three bars of the breakdown, and you're missing the fourth bar.

NOTE ▶ Logic can also continue playing in Cycle mode as you select different takes.

12 Listen to Take 1.

This time the guitarist misses the entire beginning but gives a good performance in the fourth bar of the breakdown.

Although each take is a very poor performance, you have all the material you need to create a comp take that will sound good. You will use the following sections of each take:

▶   Take 1: The fourth bar

▶   Take 2: The first and third bars

▶   Take 3: The second bar

Comping the Takes

Now you'll assemble the best sections of each take to create a single, flawless composite take using the Quick Swipe Comping feature. You will swipe your mouse across the parts of the takes you want to hear in your comp.

1   Click Take 2 to select it.

The entire take is selected, and its color and name are displayed in the take folder.

2   Click Take 3 at bar 14, and drag to the right to select one measure.

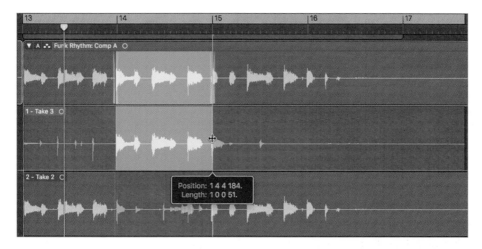

The mouse pointer does not automatically snap to the grid when Quick Swipe Comping, but snapping would help you edit this kind of rhythmic material.

Let's undo the previous selection and try repeating that operation with snapping turned on.

3   Choose Edit > Undo Edit Comp (or press Command-Z).

4   At the top of the Tracks area, from the Snap menu, choose Snap Quick Swipe Comping.

5   At bar 14, click Take 3 and drag right to select one measure.

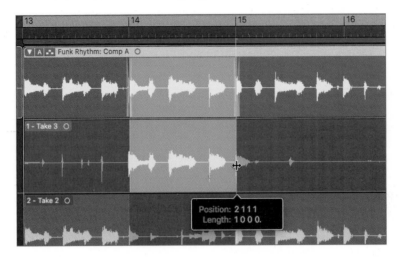

This time the mouse pointer snaps, making it easier to select exactly one measure.

6   Click Take 1 at bar 16 and drag to select one measure.

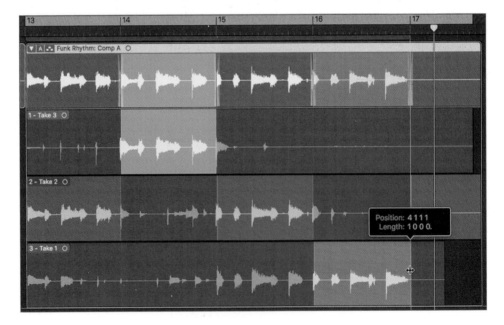

Notice that in the take folder on the Guitar track, the waveform and its background color match the sections of the selected takes. Your comp name, Comp A, now appears next to the take folder name, and the letter A is displayed in the Take Folder pop-up menu (to the right of the disclosure triangle).

NOTE ▶ A take folder can contain multiple comps that you can choose from the Take Folder pop-up menu. An easy way to start a new comp is to Option-click a take to select it, and start comping again.

7   Listen to your comp.

Although each individual guitar take was pretty poor, you've edited them together into a good-sounding guitar part. There is, however, a lingering noise present at the end of Take 2 you can delete.

8   At the end of Take 2, click the last section highlighted in blue.

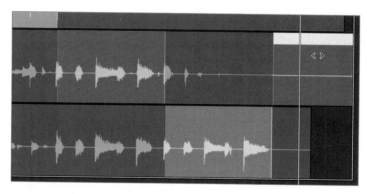

The upper part of the clicked section is white, indicating that the section is selected.

9   Press Delete to remove the selected section.

10 Listen closely to the edit at bar 16.

You can hear a double-attack on the downbeat of bar 16. You will now clean up that edit.

11 At bar 16, click-hold the right edge of the last highlighted section in take 2; then hold down Control-Shift while you drag to the left into the silent section.

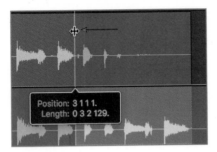

Holding Control-Shift while you drag temporarily disables the snapping, giving you the precision you need to clean up this edit.

12 From the Take Folder pop-up menu, choose Flatten.

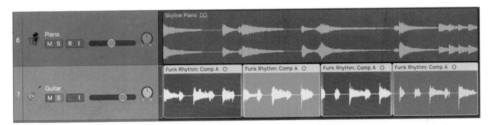

The take folder is replaced by the current comp. The selected sections of the takes in the folder are now replaced by audio regions, and crossfades are displayed at the junctions between regions.

13 Click the Guitar track's Solo button (or press S) to unsolo the track and listen to the result.

14 Turn off Cycle mode.

You now have a flawless funk rhythm guitar performance during the break. The crossfades, automatically added between edit points during the comping, ensure smooth transitions between the regions. You will learn how to apply and adjust your own fades and crossfades in the following two exercises.

Adding Fades and Crossfades

When editing audio, you usually want to avoid abrupt transitions on edit points: the region boundaries and the junctions between regions. You can use nondestructive fades in the workspace to create smooth transitions.

Adding a Fade-Out

The very last region on the Guitar track ends abruptly, before the guitar chord has finished its natural decay. You will now add a fade-out to make that last chord end more naturally.

1   Solo the Guitar track (track 7).

2   At the end of the Guitar track (at bar 21), listen to the three regions containing guitar chords.

> You can hear odd blip sounds at the edit points: the beginning of the first region, the junctions between regions, and the end of the last region. The clicks are exacerbated by the reverb in the Amp Designer plug-in on the channel strip. Let's turn off that plug-in.

3   In the inspector, on the Guitar channel strip, place the mouse pointer over the Amp Designer plug-in, and then click the power button that appears to the left of the plug-in slot.

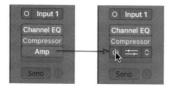

> The plug-in is dimmed to indicate that it's turned off.

4   Just above the Amp Designer plug-in, turn off the Compressor plug-in.

5   Listen again to the three guitar regions at bar 21.

> You can now clearly hear the clicks. The third region, a C minor chord, ends abruptly and the sustain tail of that chord does not sound natural.

6   Press T to open the Tool menu at the mouse pointer position.

7   Click the Fade tool, or press A, to assign it as the Left-click tool.

8   Drag the Fade tool over the end part of the *Cm chord* region, starting about halfway into the region.

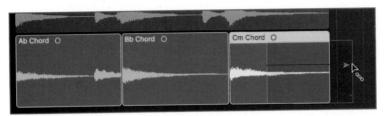

To apply a fade, always ensure that you drag over a region's boundary, or nothing will happen. You can create fades only over region boundaries. Here, the rectangular frame should cover the end of the region.

A fade-out is created. The position where you started dragging determines the length of the fade-out.

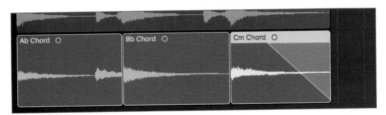

9   Listen to the fade-out.

The level of the guitar chord progressively decreases until it's silent at the end, effectively removing the click at the end of the *Cm chord* region.

TIP ▶ To remove a fade, Option-click the fade using the Fade tool.

You can now adjust the fade's length and curve to fine-tune its sound.

10 Place the Fade tool on the left side of the fade, and drag toward the left to start the fade-out at the beginning of the *Cm chord* region.

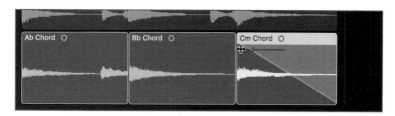

11 Place the Fade tool in the middle of the fade, and drag to the right to curve the fade.

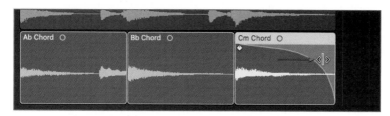

The fade is curved in the direction you drag.

12 Unsolo the Guitar track, and in the inspector, turn on the Compressor and the Amp Designer.

13 Listen to the entire outro section starting at bar 21.

The guitar and the piano fade out simultaneously at the end of the song, which now sounds cleaner and smoother.

14 Press T twice.

The Left-click tool is reassigned as the Pointer tool.

Adding Fades to Remove Clicks

In this exercise, you will add very short fades and crossfades to eliminate click sounds that occur at edit points on the final three regions on the Guitar track.

1 Solo the Guitar track, and in the inspector, turn off the Compressor and Amp Designer.

2   Listen to the *Ab chord* region at bar 21, starting playback slightly before the beginning of that region.

You can hear a click at the beginning of the region. Let's zoom in to take a closer look at the waveform.

3   Control-Option-drag around the left edge of the *Ab chord* region.

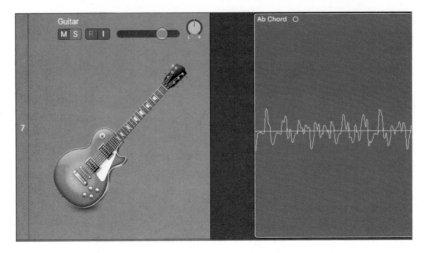

You may need to zoom in a few more times to clearly see the shape of the waveform.

To add fades using the Pointer tool, you can Control-Shift-drag over the region boundary.

4   Control-Shift-click inside the region, and drag toward the left over the region start.

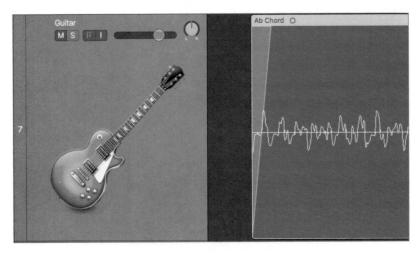

A fade-in is added.

5 Zoom out and listen to the fade-in.

The click sound at the beginning of the *Ab chord* region disappeared.

> **TIP** To compare the sound before and after the edit, choose Edit > Undo Crossfade Edit (or press Command-Z) to undo the previous edit, and choose Edit > Redo Crossfade Edit (or press Command-Shift-Z) to reapply that edit.

6 Listen to the junction between the first two regions of the outro, *Ab chord* and *Bb chord*. You can hear a click sound at the edit point.

7 Zoom in closer to the junction between the two regions, and Control-Shift-drag over the junction.

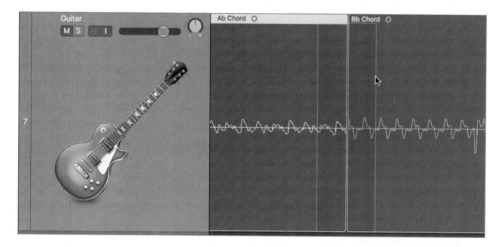

A crossfade is added at the junction between the two regions.

> **TIP** You can change the curve of a crossfade by placing the mouse pointer in the middle of the crossfade and dragging toward the left or right.

8 Zoom out and listen to the crossfade.

The click sound at the junction between the regions disappeared.

When adding short fades or crossfades to avoid clicks, you don't need to zoom in and look at the waveform. All you need is a very short fade at the edit point to smooth the transition.

There's one click left to remove: at the junction between the two final regions on the track, *Bb chord* and *Cm chord*. This time you will add the crossfade using the parameters in the Region inspector to avoid zooming in and out.

9   Click the *Bb chord* region.

10 At the top of the inspector, in the Region inspector, select the More option to display the fade parameters.

11 Double-click to the right of the Fade Out parameter to activate the data field, and enter *5*.

A five-millisecond fade-out is added at the end of the selected region.

12 Click the Type parameter value, and choose EqP (Equal Power Crossfade).

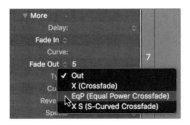

In the workspace, you can see that the fade-out at the end of the selected region is replaced by a crossfade.

NOTE ▶ While X, EqP, and X S crossfades have different shapes, the shape of EqP crossfades keeps the volume of the sound constant throughout the fade, which makes EqP the best choice for most situations.

13 Unsolo the Guitar track, turn the Compressor and Amp Designer back on, and listen to the outro.

After editing a section, you may have many small regions with fades between them. You can choose to keep those small regions with the fades so that you can readjust the edits later. However, if you are ready to commit and would rather deal with a single audio region for the entire section, you can join the regions to render your edits into a new audio file.

14 Select the *Ab*, *Bb*, and *Cm chord* regions.

15 Choose Edit > Join > Regions (or press Command-J).

An alert asks you to confirm the creation of a new audio file.

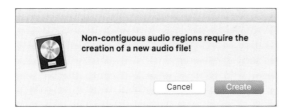

16 Click Create, or press Return.

A new audio region is created in place of the selected regions and their fades.

17 Using the Text tool, rename the new region *Gtr chords*, and then revert to the Pointer tool.

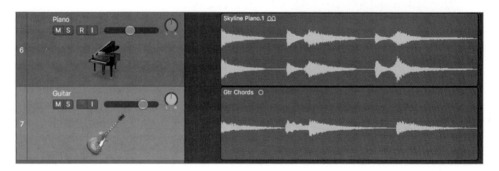

TIP▶ To rename a region without switching to the Text tool, select the region and press Shift-N.

Editing Regions in the Audio Track Editor

For some editing, you need to clearly see the grid behind the regions or have the bar ruler displayed directly on top of the regions you're editing. Zooming and scrolling in the work-space can help to an extent; however, when you want to edit the regions of a single track, you can use the Audio Track Editor to focus on that track without changing the zoom level of the Tracks area.

Importing Audio Files Using the All Files Browser

You will now import a new audio file to the project: a white noise sound effect you will use later to accentuate the transition between song sections at bar 17.

1 In the control bar, click the Browsers button (or press F).

2   At the top of the browsers, click the All Files tab.

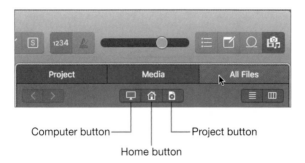

Computer button ⎯⎯⎯ ⎿⎯ Project button
Home button

The All Files Browser opens. At the top, three buttons allow you to access all the volumes connected to your computer, your home folder, or the current project folder.

3   Click the Home button.

The contents of your home folder appear in the browser.

4   Double-click Desktop, and continue double-clicking folders to navigate to Logic Pro X Files > Media > Additional Media.

5   In the All Files Browser, select **wave.aif**.

6   At the lower left of the All Files Browser, click the Play button, or press Option-Spacebar.

The **wave.aif** file plays. It's a sound effect of white noise rising and falling in level, similar to the sound of an ocean wave.

7 Drag **wave.aif** to the bottom of the workspace at bar 13.

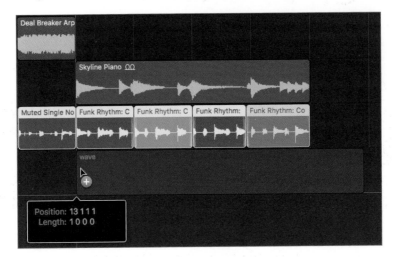

A new track is created, and the *wave* audio region is added at bar 13. The audio file was recorded at a low level, and its waveform is rather flat. Depending on your zoom level, you may not even see a waveform at all. In the next exercise, you will zoom in to the waveform so you can see it clearly.

8 In the control bar, click the Browsers button (or press F) to close the browser.

9 Play the song from bar 13 to bar 18.

The white noise effect sounds like it will work in that section. However, for maximum effect, it must be positioned so that the climax of the wave sound occurs at bar 17.

Using the Audio Track Editor

You will now continue editing the *wave* region nondestructively, but this time in the Audio Track Editor, which allows you to clearly see the grid and the ruler above the regions without having to change the zoom level of the Tracks area.

1 In the workspace, double-click the *wave* region to open the editors area.

2   At the top of the editors area, click Track.

The Audio Track Editor opens, displaying the wave track and its single region.

3   Press Z.

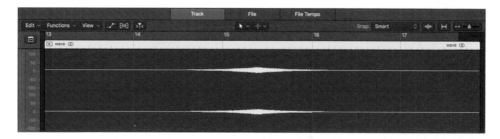

The *wave* region fills the Audio Track Editor. You can clearly see the ruler just above the waveform, with vertical grid lines displayed under the waveform.

You can see that the *wave* region is a stereo audio region because it has two interleaved circles next to its name, and two waveforms are displayed in the Audio Track Editor.

NOTE ▶ In the workspace, when stereo audio regions zoomed out, they appear as a single waveform. As you reach a certain zoom level, two waveforms are displayed, one for each channel.

Let's zoom in on the waveform.

4   At the top right of the Audio Track Editor, click the Waveform Zoom button.

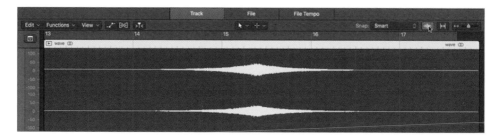

The waveform is a little taller. Let's zoom in even closer.

5   Click and hold down the Waveform Zoom button until the vertical zoom slider appears, and then drag up until you can clearly see the waveform.

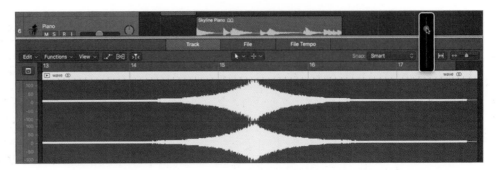

NOTE ▶ A separate Waveform Zoom button at the upper right of the Tracks area allows you to adjust the vertical zoom level of audio region waveforms in the workspace.

6   In the Audio Track Editor, drag the *wave* region to the right until the highest point on the waveform is aligned with bar 17.

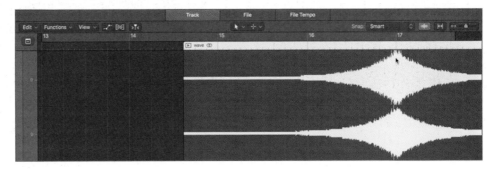

In the workspace, the *wave* audio region is moved accordingly.

7   In the Tracks area, position the playhead before the *wave* region, and press the Space-bar to play the results.

The climax of the wave sound is now perfectly aligned with the transition between song sections at bar 17. The effect would sound even better if the rise before bar 17 were shorter.

8   Stop playback.

9 In the Audio Track Editor, place the mouse pointer at the lower left of the *wave* region until it turns into the Resize tool. Then drag to the right so the region starts at bar 16.

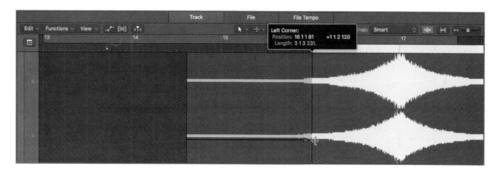

The region is now trimmed. Let's add a fade-in.

10 In the Audio Track Editor, Control-Shift-click the waveform at bar 17 and drag toward the left over the region start.

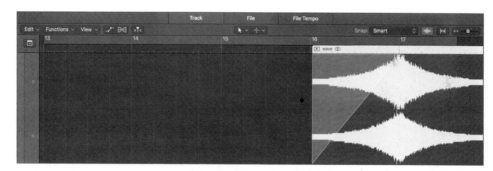

A fade-in is added. All the edits you perform in the Audio Track Editor are reflected in the workspace.

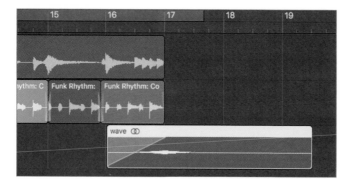

11 In the control bar, click the Editors button (or press E) to close the Audio Track Editor.

12 Listen to the song from the beginning of the breakdown at bar 11.

The wave sound now rises rapidly in the last bar of the breakdown and decays slowly in the next section, which works better for this transition.

Playing an Audio Region Backward

You will now create a new region from the last chord of the *Gtr chords* region at the end of the Guitar track, and copy it to the beginning of the song. You will then reverse the new audio region to create a swelling sound effect during the introduction.

1 On the Guitar track, Command-drag the last bar of the *Gtr chords* region to select it with the Marquee tool.

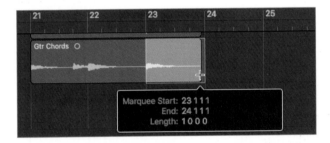

You will now copy that region to bar 4, the last bar of the introduction.

2 Option-drag the region to the left, and release the mouse button when the help tag displays Position: 4 1 1 1.

You have a new *Gtr chords.3* region in the introduction that you will reverse nondestructively.

3 At bar 4, ensure that the new *Gtr chords.3* region is still selected, and in the Region inspector, select Reverse.

In the Tracks area, you can see the *Gtr chords.3* region's waveform being reversed: it starts with silence and slowly builds up to the sustained guitar chord.

4   Press the Spacebar to listen to the introduction.

The swelling guitar chord sounds about right. But it's still not in the perfect position because it overlaps the first notes of the bass. To get the full impact of the break at the end of the intro, the *Gtr chords.3* region should end exactly where the first *Skyline Bass* region starts.

5   From the Snap menu, choose Smart.

6   Drag the *Gtr chords.3* region a little toward the left.

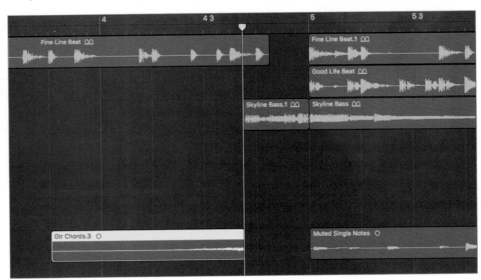

To help line up the end of the reversed guitar with the first notes on the bass track, you can zoom in horizontally and position the playhead at the beginning of the *Skyline Bass.1* region.

Now the swelling guitar chord sounds smooth. It catches the listener's attention just before the bass first comes in, accentuating the effect of the break at the end of the introduction.

Aligning Audio

Accurately aligning audio material to the grid, or to other instruments in the song, is crucial to realizing a professional-sounding song. No amount of plug-ins, mixing, or mastering techniques can fix a sloppy arrangement, so getting a tight-sounding arrangement before moving on is important.

You will now import a guitar recording that was removed from the workspace but kept in the Project Audio Browser. That guitar was removed because of timing issues, which you can now fix using the Flex tool.

1   In the control bar, click the Browsers button (or press F).

2   At the top of the browser, click the Project tab.

3   In the Project Audio Browser, scroll all the way down, and then drag the *Guitar Intro* region to the Guitar track at bar 1.

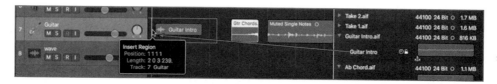

4   Click the Browsers button (or press F) to close the Project Audio Browser.

5   Play the introduction that includes your new *Guitar Intro* region.

The guitarist is playing four dead notes (unpitched percussive sounds when the string wasn't ringing) that cause a ringing in the vintage spring reverb in the guitar amp modeling plug-in.

The third note, at bar 2, sounds out of place, while the other notes play at the second and fourth beat of each bar, much as a snare would be heard in a drum pattern. You will move that third dead note to the second beat of bar 2.

6   Press T, and choose the Flex tool, or press X.

7   Using the Flex tool, click anywhere on the *Guitar Intro* region.

The audio files used on the Guitar track are analyzed for transients. You may see a progress window briefly.

NOTE ▶ When you click an audio region using the Flex tool, Logic automatically chooses a flex mode and analyzes all audio files on the same track to detect their transients. You will learn more about flex editing in Lesson 7.

8   Zoom in closer on the *Guitar Intro* region so that you can see the ruler above the waveform (or press Z).

9   Place the Flex tool over the attack of the third note (at bar 2).

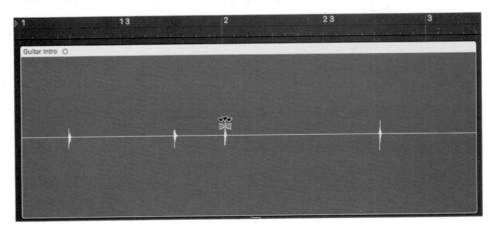

Depending on its position over the waveform, the Flex tool can perform different functions, indicated by different tool icons. So make sure that the tool is located precisely over the note's attack and looks like the pointer icon in the preceding figure.

10 Drag the Flex tool to the right to move the third guitar note to measure 2, beat 2.

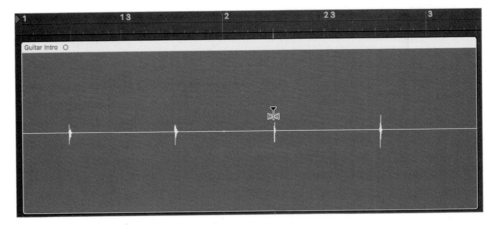

11 Play the introduction.

The dead notes in the first two bars now sound consistent.

The dead notes in this guitar region are still not located perfectly on the grid. If you wanted to take this a little further, you could set your snap mode to Beat, zoom in closer on the first guitar note, and use the Flex tool to drag it exactly on the beat. Then you'd repeat this operation on the second and fourth notes.

You now know how to read a waveform, identifying notes and their attacks to perform precise and clean edits. You acquired skills with a number of editing tools—such as the Marquee tool, Fade tool, Resize tool, Flex tool, take folders, and snap modes—that you will continue to use as you edit recordings and arrange projects.

Further, you can now accelerate your workflow by choosing the appropriate Left-click and Command-click tools for each job. As you produce more music in Logic, you will continue sharpening those skills in the course of becoming an increasingly proficient audio engineer.

Lesson Review

1. What is nondestructive audio editing?
2. Where can you perform nondestructive editing?
3. How do you comp takes?
4. How do you prepare to edit the takes inside a take folder?
5. How can you see the result of your comp as regions?
6. How do you add a fade-in or fade-out to a region?
7. How do you add a crossfade between two regions?
8. How do you select a section of an audio region?
9. Which tool allows you to move an individual note inside an audio region without dividing the region?

Answers

1. Audio region editing that does not alter the audio data in the referenced audio file
2. In the workspace or in the Audio Track Editor
3. Open the take folder, and drag over each take to highlight the desired sections. The take folder assembles a comp including all the highlighted sections.
4. Click the Quick Swipe Comping button at the top left of the take folder to disable Quick Swipe Comping mode.
5. From the Take Folder pop-up menu, choose Flatten.
6. Drag the Fade tool over the boundaries of a region (or Control-Shift-drag the Pointer tool), or adjust the Fade In parameter in the Region inspector.

7.   Drag the Fade tool over the junction of the regions (or Control-Shift-drag the Pointer tool), or adjust the Fade Out parameter in the Region inspector.

8.   Use the Marquee tool.

9.   The Flex tool

Keyboard Shortcuts

Workspace

Control-Shift-drag with the Pointer tool	Adds a fade
Option-click with the Fade tool	Removes a fade
While dragging, press and hold down Control	Partially disables snapping
While dragging, press and hold down Control-Shift	Disables snapping with increased placement precision
Command-J	Renders the selected regions and their fades into a single new audio region
Command-G	Toggles snapping to grid

Tools

T	Opens the Tool menu at the mouse pointer position
Press T twice	Changes the Left-click tool to a pointer

Working with
Virtual Instruments

4

Time

Goals

This lesson takes approximately 75 minutes to complete.

Create a new project with a Drummer track

Choose a drummer and drum kit

Edit the drummer performance

Arrange the song structure

Edit performances in the new sections

Customize the drum kit

Tune and dampen individual kit pieces

Work with electronic drummers

Customize drum machines

Convert Drummer regions to MIDI regions

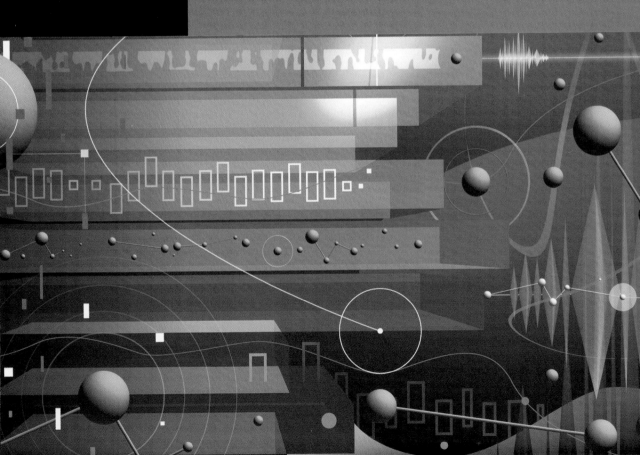

Lesson **4**

Producing a Virtual Drum Track

In most popular modern music genres, drums are the backbone of the instrumentation. They provide the foundation for the tempo and groove of the piece. For recording sessions in which the instruments are not tracked at the same time, drums are usually recorded or programmed first so that the other musicians can record while listening to their rhythmic reference.

To meet today's high production standards, producing drum tracks usually involves using several techniques, including live recording, programming, sampling, audio quantizing, and sound replacement. In Logic Pro X, you can speed up the process by taking advantage of the Drummer feature along with its companion software instruments, Drum Kit Designer and Drum Machine Designer.

In this lesson, you will produce virtual indie-rock, hip-hop, and electro-house drum tracks. After selecting a genre and choosing the best drummer for your project, you will adjust the drummer's performance, making her play busier patterns or simpler ones, louder or softer, and changing the feel, almost like a producer would communicate with a real drummer in a recording session.

Creating a Drummer Track

Drummer is a Logic Pro X feature that allows you to produce drum tracks using a virtual drummer with its own personal playing style. Its performance is placed in Drummer regions on a Drummer track. Using the Drummer Editor, you can edit the performance data contained in a Drummer region. Each virtual drummer also comes with its own drum kit software instrument plug-ins: Drum Kit Designer or Drum Machine Designer (which controls Ultrabeat in the background).

First, let's open a new project, add a Drummer track, and examine the display of the drum performance in the Drummer region.

1   Choose File > New (or press Command-Shift-N).

A new project opens along with the New Tracks dialog.

2   In the New Tracks dialog, select Drummer, make sure the Genre pop-up menu is set to Rock, and click Create.

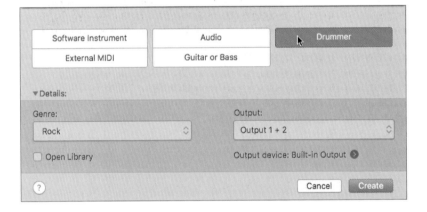

A Drummer track is created along with an eight-bar Drummer region. At the bottom of the main window, the Drummer Editor opens, allowing you to edit the performance in the Drummer region that is selected in the workspace. The track is named

SoCal (Kyle), which is the name of the default drum kit and default virtual drummer in the Rock category. The project tempo is set to 110 bpm, which suits the selected music genre.

Drummer region

Drummer Editor

3   Press the Spacebar to listen to the Drummer region.

The drummer starts with a crash cymbal and plays a straightforward rock pattern. At the end of the Drummer region, a drum fill leads into the next section, which you will add later.

Let's take a closer look at the Drummer region.

4   Control-Option-drag over the first bar of the Drummer region. If necessary, continue zooming vertically by dragging the vertical zoom slider (or pressing Command-Down Arrow) until you can see two lanes in the Drummer region.

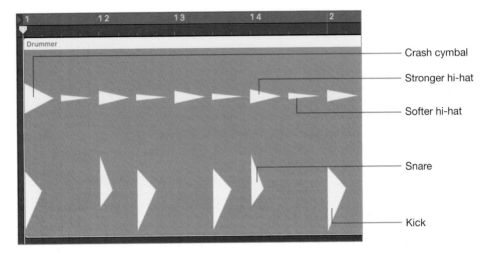

The Drummer region displays drum hits as triangles on lanes, roughly emulating the look of drum hits on an audio waveform. Kicks and snares are shown on the bottom lane; cymbals, toms, and hand percussions are on the top lane.

5   In the upper half of the ruler, drag a one-measure cycle area at bar 1.

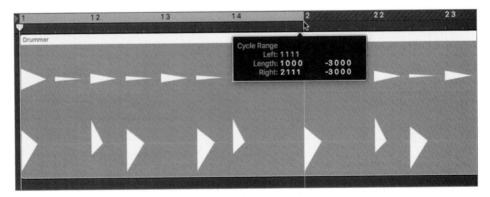

6   Listen to the first bar a few times while looking at the drum hits in the Drummer region.

Although you cannot edit individual drum hits in the Drummer region, the region display gives you a quick glance at the drummer's performance.

MORE INFO ▶ At the end of this lesson you will convert Drummer regions to MIDI regions. In Lesson 6, you will learn how to edit MIDI regions.

7 Turn off Cycle mode.

8 In the workspace, click the background and press Z to zoom out and see the entire drummer region.

Now you can read the Drummer region. In the next exercise, you will listen to multiple drummers and several performance presets. Later, you will zoom in again to see the Drummer region update as you adjust its settings in the Drummer Editor.

Choosing a Drummer and a Style

Each drummer has his own playing style and drum kit, and those combine to create a unique drum sound. Before you start fine-tuning the drummer's performance, you need to choose the right drummer for the song.

In the Library, drummers are categorized by music genres. By default, choosing a new drummer means loading a new virtual drum kit and updating Drummer region settings. But sometimes you may want to keep the same drum kit while changing the drummer, which you will do in this exercise.

1 In the Control bar, click the Library button.

The Library lets you access drummers and drum kit patches.

2 Place the mouse pointer over Anders.

A help tag describes that drummer's playing style and the sound of his drum kit. Let's get to know the other drummers.

3   Continue by placing the pointer over other rock drummers to read their descriptions. When you're through, click the drummer named Jesse.

In the Library, Jesse's drum kit Smash is selected. In the workspace, the Drummer region updates to display Jesse's performance.

4   In the workspace, click the Drummer region to select it.

The Drummer Editor shows the settings for the selected Drummer region. A yellow ruler allows you to position the playhead anywhere within the region, and you can click the Play button to the left of the ruler to preview the Drummer region. As in the Tracks area, you can also double-click the ruler to start and stop playback.

5   In the Drummer Editor, click the Play button.

Play button   Playhead

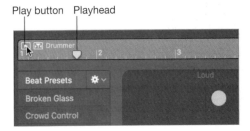

The selected region plays in Cycle mode, and the cycle area automatically matches the region position and length. The selected region is soloed—indicated by a thin yellow frame. Soloing the region helps you focus on the drums when you have other tracks in the project.

Although you will later fine-tune the drummer's performance, Jesse's busy, syncopated drum patterns are not a good fit for this indie-rock song. You are looking for a drummer with a simple, straightforward style that more appropriately serves the song.

6   Stop playback.

In the Tracks area, Cycle mode is automatically turned off, the dimmed cycle area returns to its original position and length, and the selected region is no longer soloed.

7 In the Library, click the Alternative category and click the first drummer, Aidan.

8 In the Drummer Editor, click the Play button.

While the region is playing back in Cycle mode, you can try selecting other region settings presets to explore Aidan's full range of playing style.

9 In the Presets column, click a few different presets while the region plays back.

When you click a preset, the region settings update and you can hear another performance from the same drummer.

10 Without stopping playback, in the Library, choose the Rock category.

11 Click the fourth drummer, Max – Punk Rock. If a dialog explaining how to keep region settings when changing the drummer appears, select "do not show this message again," and click Change Drummer. Listen to a few of Max's presets.

Although Max's hyperactive performance is not what you're looking for, the drum kit sounds punchy. Let's assign the first drummer, Kyle, to play on Max's drum kit, East Bay.

12 In the Library, click the padlock icon in the Sounds section.

The current patch is locked, and changing the drummer will no longer load a new drum kit.

13 In the Library, click Kyle.

Kyle is now playing Max's East Bay drum kit. Let's make him play a bit faster.

14 In the control bar, set the tempo to 142 bpm.

15 Stop playback.

You have found a drummer that plays the straightforward style you're seeking for this project, paired a punchy-sounding drum kit, and set a tempo that will drive your indie-rock song. You are now ready to customize the performance.

Editing the Drum Performance

In a recording session with a live drummer, the artist, the producer, or the musical director must communicate their vision of the completed song. They may ask the drummer to play behind or ahead of the beat to change the feel of the groove, switch from the hi-hat to the ride cymbal during the chorus, or play a drum fill in a specific location.

In Logic Pro X, editing a drummer performance is almost like giving instructions to a real drummer. In this exercise, you will play a drum region in Cycle mode as you adjust the drummer settings.

1   In the workspace, make sure the Drummer region is still selected, and in the Drummer Editor, click the Play button.

    Next to the presets, an XY pad with a yellow puck lets you adjust both the loudness and the complexity of the drum pattern.

2   As the region plays, drag the puck, or click different locations inside the pad to reposition it.

TIP ▶ To undo a Drummer Editor adjustment, press Command-Z.

After positioning the puck, you must wait for the region to update (update time varies depending on your computer). If you drag the puck constantly, the region will not update.

As you position the puck farther to the right, the drum pattern becomes more complex, and as you move the puck toward the top of the pad, the drummer plays louder. Try placing the puck in the pad's corners for extreme settings, such as soft and simple or loud and complex.

As the drummer plays softer, he closes the hi-hat and switches from hitting the snare drum on the skin to playing rim clicks (hitting only the rim of the drum). As he plays louder, he opens the hi-hat and start playing rim shots (hitting the skin and the rim simultaneously for accent).

Let's make the drummer play a solid, straightforward beat in the Drummer region, which will be used for the first verse of the song.

3   Settle for a puck position where the drummer plays a rather simple and fairly loud pattern.

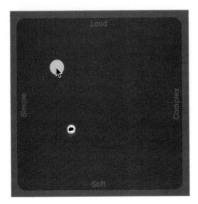

The kick drum is still playing a pattern that's a bit too busy. To the right of the XY pad, you can choose from several Kick & Snare pattern variations.

4   Drag the Kick & Snare slider to position 2 (or click the second increment on the slider).

TIP ▶ In multitrack projects, when you select the Follow checkbox, a pop-up menu appears instead of the Kick & Snare slider. The menu lets you choose a track to influence what the drummer plays on the kick and snare.

The drummer now simply alternates kick and snare on every beat. If you don't hear the drummer play the snare on beats 2 and 4, slightly readjust the horizontal position of the puck in the XY pad so it's in the same position as in the figure following step 3.

Listen to the hi-hat. It is currently playing eighth notes.

5   Click the first increment on the Hi-Hat slider.

The hi-hat now plays only on the beat (quarter notes), which works well for up-tempo songs.

The drummer is playing a fill in the middle of the region (before bar 5) and another at the end (before bar 9). Let's get rid of the first fill and keep only one at the end.

6   Look at the region in the workspace while trying different positions for the Fills knob, and drag the Fills knob down until you see the fill before bar 5 disappear. You should still see a fill at the end of the region.

NOTE ▶ Clicking the small lock icon next to the Fills and Swing knobs locks the knob into position as you preview presets or drummers.

TIP ▶ Each time you adjust a setting in the Drummer Editor, the selected region is refreshed, and the drummer plays a new subtle variation. Dragging the Fills knob by a tiny amount is a quick way to refresh a region. You can also click the Action pop-up menu next to the Presets menu and choose Refresh Region. Or you can Control-click the region in the workspace, and from the shortcut menu, choose Edit > Refresh Region.

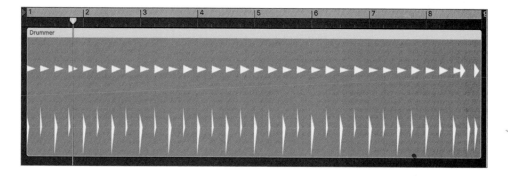

You now have a very straightforward beat. Because the drummer plays less now, he can make the hi-hat ring a bit more.

7   In the Drummer Editor, click the Details button to display three knobs.

8   Below the Hi-Hat knob, deselect the Automatic option.

9   Drag the Hi-Hat knob up to open it a little bit.

This verse's drum pattern now sounds great, so let's add a new Drummer region, which you'll use for the chorus.

10 Stop playback.

11 In the Tracks area, adjust your zoom level to see some empty space after the Drummer region, position the mouse cursor over the Drummer track, and click the + sign that appears to the right of the Drummer region.

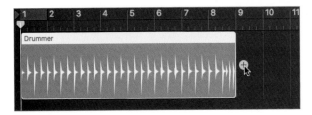

A new eight-bar Drummer region is created at bar 9. The new region is selected, and the Drummer Editor displays its region settings, the same as the original Drummer region on the track. Let's make the drummer switch from playing the hi-hat to playing a cymbal during the chorus.

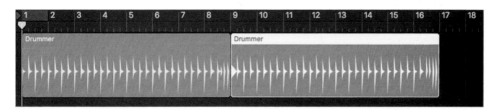

12 In the Drummer Editor, click the Play button.

You can hear the second region in Cycle mode.

13 In the Drummer editor, click the Details button to go back to the basic view.

14 On the drum kit, click a cymbal.

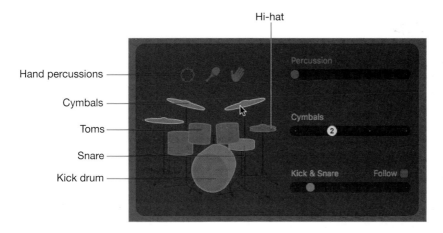

The hi-hat is dimmed, the cymbals are yellow, and you can hear the drummer play a ride cymbal instead of the hi-hat. The drummer is playing the ride cymbal on every eighth note. For a more powerful chorus, you instead want it to play crash cymbals on every beat.

15 Click the first increment of the Cymbals slider.

You now hear crash cymbals on every beat and the beat has more impact.

Let's listen to the verse going into the chorus.

16 Stop playback.

17 Go to the beginning of the song and listen to both Drummer regions.

You now have a simple, straightforward beat for the verse, and then the drummer switches to the crash cymbal for the busier chorus pattern.

You have carefully crafted two eight-measure drum grooves: one for the verse and one for the chorus. They are the two most important building blocks of the song you will now start arranging.

Arranging the Drum Track

In this exercise, you will lay out the song structure and populate the Drummer track with Drummer regions for the whole song.

Using Markers in the Arrangement Track

Using the Arrangement track, you will now create arrangement markers for all the sections of your song. You'll adjust their lengths, positions, and order, and fill all the new sections with Drummer regions.

1   At the top of the track headers, click the Global Tracks button (or press G).

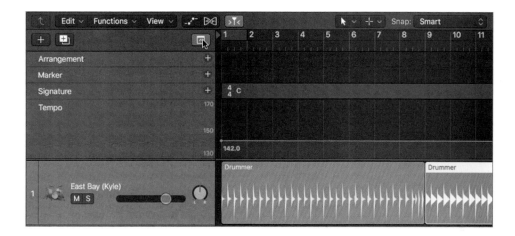

The global tracks open, with the Arrangement track at the top. You won't need the other global tracks, so you can hide them.

2   Control-click a global track header, and choose Configure Global Tracks (or press Option-G).

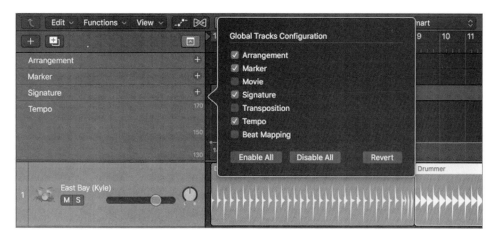

A shortcut menu opens in which you select the global tracks you want to display.

3   Deselect the Marker, Signature, and Tempo tracks, and click outside the shortcut menu to close it.

The Arrangement track is now closer to the regions in the workspace, making it easier to see their relationships.

4   In the Arrangement track header, click the Add Marker button (+).

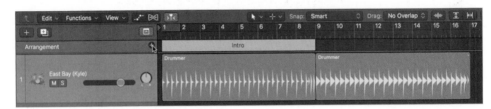

An eight-measure arrangement marker named Intro is created at the beginning of the song. By default, arrangement markers are eight bars long and are placed one after the other, starting from the beginning of the song. Let's rename the marker.

5   Click the name of the marker, and from the menu, choose Verse.

6   Click the Add Marker button (+) to create a new marker, and make sure it's named Chorus.

You will now create a marker for a new intro section and insert it before the Verse and Chorus markers.

7   In the Arrangement track header, click the Add Marker (+) button.

An eight-bar marker is created.

8   Click the name of the new marker, and from the pop-up menu, choose Intro.

A four-measure intro will be long enough, so you can resize the Intro marker before moving it.

9   Drag the right edge of the Intro marker toward the left to shorten it to four bars.

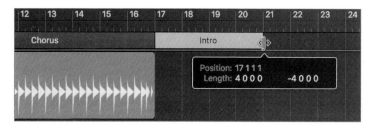

10 Click the marker away from its name (to avoid opening the Name pop-up menu), and
    drag the Intro marker to bar 1.

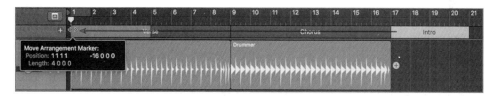

The Intro marker is inserted at bar 1, and the Verse and Chorus markers move to the
right of the new Intro section. In the workspace, the Drummer regions move along
with their respective arrangement markers.

As with regions in the workspace, you can Option-drag a marker to copy it.

11 Press Command-Left Arrow to zoom out horizontally and make space to the right
    of the existing song sections. Option-drag the Verse marker to bar 21, right after the
    chorus.

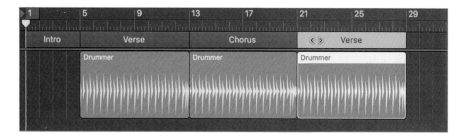

The Verse marker and the Drummer region are copied together.

12 Option-drag the Chorus marker to bar 29, after the second verse.

The Chorus marker and the Drummer region are copied together.

The song is taking shape. You will now finish arranging the song structure with a bridge, a chorus, and an outro section. As you place the last three markers, continue zooming out horizontally as necessary.

13 In the Arrangement track header, click the Add Marker (+) button.

A Bridge marker is created after the last chorus.

14 Click the Add Marker (+) button two more times to create markers for the Chorus and Outro sections.

15 Make sure the two last markers have the correct names, Chorus and Outro.

Let's shorten the outro section a bit.

16 Resize the Outro marker to make it four bars long.

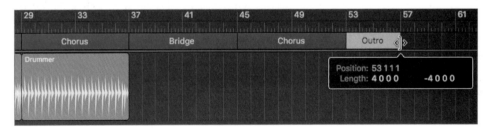

The song structure is now complete, and you can add Drummer regions to fill out the empty sections.

17 On the Drummer track, Control-click the background and choose Populate with Drummer Regions.

New Drummer regions are created for all the empty arrangement markers.

18 Listen to the drum track, focusing on the new sections.

New patterns were automatically created for each new Drummer region.

TIP ▶ To delete all the regions below an arrangement marker, select the marker, and press Delete. To remove the arrangement marker, press Delete again.

Amazing as the playing is, Kyle (the drummer) might not have guessed what you had in mind for each section. You will now edit some of the new regions to adjust the drummer's performance.

Editing the Intro Drum Performance

In this exercise, you will make the drummer play the hi-hat instead of the toms. Later, you'll cut the Intro region in two so that you can use different settings for the second part of the intro and make the drummer play a progressively louder and more complex pattern.

1 In the workspace, click the background to deselect all regions, and click the Intro region to select it.

The Drummer Editor shows its settings.

Throughout this exercise you can click the Play button in the Drummer Editor to start and stop playback, or you can navigate the workspace by pressing the Spacebar (Play or Stop) and the Return key (Go to Beginning).

2 Listen to the Intro.

Let's make the drummer play the hi-hat instead of the toms.

3 In the Drummer Editor, click the hi-hat.

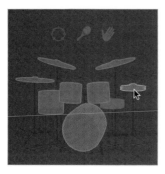

When you click the hi-hat, the toms are muted automatically. Aside from the kick and snare, the drummer can focus on the toms, the hi-hat, or the cymbals (ride and crash).

The drums are still a little too loud and busy for this intro.

4 In the XY pad, drag the puck toward the bottom left.

The drums are softer, but the transition into the first verse at bar 5 is a little abrupt. Making the drums play crescendo (increasingly louder) during the intro will help build up some tension leading into that verse. To make the loudness evolve throughout the intro, you will cut the Intro region in two.

5 Stop playback.

6 Hold down Command to use the Marquee tool, and double-click the Intro region at bar 3.

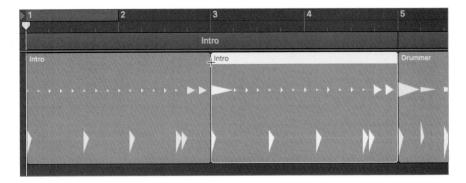

The region is divided into two two-measure regions. When a region is divided, the drummer automatically adapts his performance, and plays a fill at the end of each new region.

7 Select the first Intro region.

8 In the Drummer Editor, drag the Fills knob all the way down.

Notice how the crash disappears from the first beat of the following region. Even though it is in another region, the crash is actually a part of the fill. Now let's create the crescendo.

9 Select the second Intro region, and in the XY pad, drag the puck up to make the drummer play louder.

10 Listen to the whole intro going into the first verse.

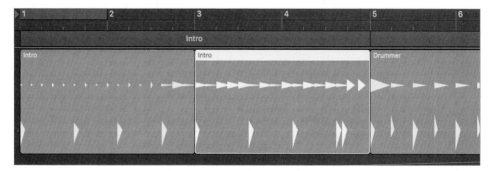

The drummer automatically starts playing louder before the end of the first intro region, which transitions into the louder second region and creates a nice tension at the start of the song. At bar 5, a crash punctuates the fill at the end of the intro. The straightforward groove continues in the Verse section, with the hi-hat a little less open to leave space to later add a singer.

Editing the Bridge Drum Performance

In a song, the bridge serves to break the sequence of alternating verses and choruses. Often, the main idea of the song is exposed in the choruses, and verses help support or develop that statement. The bridge can present an alternate idea, a different point of view. Departing from the main idea of the song increases the listener's appreciation for returning to the chorus at the end of the song—almost like taking a vacation can increase your appreciation for going back home.

For this fast, high-energy indie-rock song, a quieter bridge in which the instruments play softer will offer a refreshing dynamic contrast. Playing softer does not mean the instruments have to play less, however. In fact, you will make the drums play a busier pattern during this bridge.

1   Listen to the Bridge region.

> **TIP** ▶ When pressing the Spacebar to play a section, you can use Cycle mode to ensure that playback always starts at the beginning of the section. Drag a section's arrangement marker into the ruler to turn on Cycle mode and create a cycle area that matches the section.

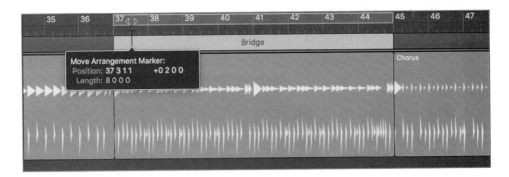

The drummer plays at the same level as in the previous sections, but he plays more here. You need to bring down the energy level.

2   Select the Bridge Drummer region.

3   In the XY pad, position the puck farther down and all the way to the right.

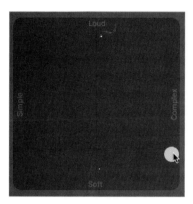

The drummer is still playing a lot, but he's much quieter. To take this bridge into a different tonal direction, you want Kyle to play toms.

4   On the drum kit, mute the snare and unmute the toms.

The hi-hat is muted automatically when you unmute the toms.

Let's choose a busier pattern for the toms.

5   On the Toms slider, click increment 3.

Kyle is now playing sixteenth notes on the toms, which creates a mysterious vibe similar to tribal percussion.

Kyle plays slightly ahead of the beat during the bridge. However, the timing nuance is subtle, and it's difficult to hear without other instruments to compare with Kyle's timing. Let's turn on the metronome and experiment with the feel of the performance.

6   In the control bar, click the Metronome button (or press K).

7   In the Drummer Editor, click the Details button to display the three setting knobs.

8   Try setting different positions of the Feel knob, and then listen to the results.

Listen to the way the drums play compared to the metronome. Don't be afraid to drag the Feel knob all the way up or down to hear the effect of extreme Feel settings.

▶   Dragging the Feel knob toward Push makes the drummer play ahead of the beat. He sounds as if he's rushing, thereby creating a sense of urgency.

▶   Dragging the Feel knob toward Pull makes the drummer play behind the beat. He sounds as if he's lazy or late, and the groove is more relaxed.

Settle on a Feel knob position more toward Pull to realize a reasonably relaxed groove.

9   Click the Details button to hide the three setting knobs.

10   Turn off Cycle mode.

11   In the control bar, click the Metronome button (or press K) to turn it off.

You have radically changed the drummer's performance in that region. Kyle now plays the bridge with a busy tribal pattern on the toms. He uses restraint, hitting softly and behind the beat, with a slight crescendo toward the end. The quiet and laid-back yet complex drum groove brings a welcome pause to an otherwise high-energy drum performance, and builds up tension leading into the last two sections.

Editing the Chorus and Outro Sections

You will now finish editing the drummer's performance by adjusting the settings of the last two chorus and outro drummer regions in your workspace.

1   Select the Chorus region after the bridge and listen to it.

That Chorus region was created when you populated the track with Drummer regions earlier in this lesson. It doesn't have the same settings as the previous two choruses and sounds busier, except for Kyle playing the ride cymbal instead of the crash.

2   On the Cymbals slider, click the first increment.

The drummer now plays the crash, and this last chorus is more consistent with the previous two choruses.

3   Select the Outro region at the end of the track and listen to it.

The drummer plays a loud beat, heavy on the crash, which could work for an outro. You will, however, make it play double-time (twice as fast) to end the song in a big way.

4   On the Kick & Snare slider, click the last increment (8).

Now it sounds like you've unleashed Kyle! Playing double-time at that fast tempo makes the sixteenth notes on the kick drum sound ridiculously fast.

5   On the XY pad, drag the puck toward the left until the drummer stops playing sixteenth notes on the kick drum.

The performance now sounds more realistic while retaining the driving effect of its double-time groove.

6   Listen to the last chorus and the outro.

The outro has the required power to drive the last four measures; however, it seems like the drummer stops abruptly before finishing the fill. Usually drummers end a song by playing the last note on the first beat of a new bar, but here a crash cymbal is missing on the downbeat at bar 57. You will resize the last Outro region in the workspace to accommodate that last drum hit.

7   Resize the last Outro region to lengthen it by one beat (until the help tag reads Length: 4 1 0 0 +0 1 0 0).

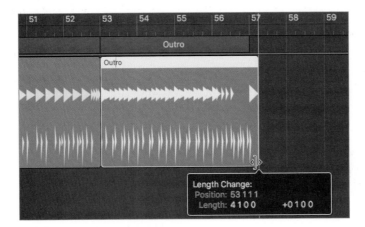

A moment after you release the mouse button, the Drummer region updates, and you can see a kick and a crash on the downbeat at bar 57.

8   Listen to the outro. The drummer finishes the fill, punctuating it with the last hit at bar 57.

> **NOTE ▶** The final crash cymbal continues ringing until its natural sustain fades out, well after the playhead has passed the end of the last Outro region.

You've laid out the entire song structure by creating section markers in the arrangement track, populated each section with Drummer regions, and edited each region's settings to customize its drum pattern. You are now done editing the drum performance and can focus on the sound of the drums.

Customizing the Drum Kit

When recording a live drummer in a studio, the engineer often positions microphones on each drum. This allows control over the recorded sound of each drum, so he can individually equalize or compress the sound of each kit piece. The producer may also want the drummer to try different kicks or snares, or to experiment with hitting the cymbals softer before he begins recording.

In Logic, when using Drummer, the sounds of each drum are already recorded. However, you can still use several tools to customize the drum kit and adjust the sound of each drum.

Adjusting the Drum Levels Using Smart Controls

Smart Controls are a set of knobs and switches that are premapped to the most important parameters of the plug-ins on the channel strip of the selected track. You will study Smart Controls in more detail in Lesson 5.

In this exercise, you will use Smart Controls to quickly adjust the levels and tones of different drums. Then you'll open Drum Kit Designer to swap one snare for another and fine-tune the crash cymbal sound.

1 In the control bar, click the Smart Controls button (or press B).

The Smart Controls pane opens at the bottom of the main window, replacing the Drummer Editor. It is divided into three sections: Mix, Compression, and Effects.

In the Mix section, six knobs allow you to balance the levels of the drums. To the right of each knob, a button lets you mute the corresponding drum or group of drums.

2 Position the playhead before the first chorus and start playback.

3 Turn the cymbals down a bit by dragging the Cymbals knob.

Even with the Amount knob turned all the way down in the Compression section, the compressor is still slightly processing the drum sound. Let's turn it off.

4   In the Compression section, click the On button.

On the left channel strip in the inspector, the Compressor plug-in is dimmed, indicating that it is turned off.

5   In the Effects section, drag the Tone knob up.

As you drag up the knob, the drums' sound changes timbre and becomes brighter. On the left channel strip in the inspector, the EQ curve on the channel strip's EQ display reflects the changes made to the Channel EQ plug-in.

 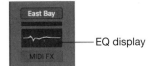

MORE INFO ▶ You will further examine the Channel EQ plug-in in Lesson 9.

6   Drag up the Room knob.

As you drag up the knob, you will start hearing the subtle reverberation of a drum booth. In the inspector, you can see the Bus 1 Send knob move along with the Tone knob.

MORE INFO ▶ You will learn how to use bus sends to route an audio signal to a reverb and to change the character of the reverb in Lesson 9.

7 In the control bar, click the Editors button (or press E) to open the Drummer Editor.

TIP You can also double-click a Drummer region to open the Drummer Editor.

You have adjusted the levels and timbres of the drums, and you're now ready to fine-tune the sound of the individual drum kit pieces.

Customizing the Kit with Drum Kit Designer

Drum Kit Designer is a software instrument plug-in that plays drum samples triggered by Drummer. It allows you to customize the drum kit by choosing from a collection of drums and cymbals and tuning and dampening them.

1 In the inspector, click in the middle of the Drum Kit Designer plug-in slot to open the plug-in.

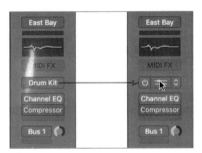

TIP To have the Drummer regions play a different instrument, you can choose another patch from the Library or insert another software instrument plug-in on the channel strip. You can also drag Drummer regions to another software instrument track, and they are automatically converted to MIDI regions. (You will learn more about MIDI in Lesson 5.)

2   In Drum Kit Designer, click the snare.

You can hear the snare sample. The snare stays lit, and the rest of the drum kit is in shadow. To the left, a Snares panel contains your choice of three snare drums, and to the right, an Edit panel includes three setting knobs.

The left panel shows only a limited selection of snares. To gain access to the entire collection of drum samples included with Logic Pro X, you need to choose a Producer Kit in the Library.

TIP To trigger Drum Kit Designer from your iPad in Logic Remote, tap the View menu and then tap Kits (you will learn how to use the Logic Remote app in Appendix A).

3   In the control bar, click the Library button (or press Y).

To the left of the inspector, the Library opens, listing patches for the selected track. The current patch, East Bay, is selected.

4   In the Library, select Producer Kits, and then select East Bay+.

The plug-in window now displays a Channel EQ plug-in. Let's reopen Drum Kit Designer.

5   Close the Channel EQ plug-in window.

6   At the top of the Library, click the drum kit icon.

The Drum Kit Designer plug-in window opens. The East Bay+ kit sounds the same as East Bay but allows a wide array of options to customize the drum kit and its mix.

MORE INFO ▸ In the track header, you may have noticed that the drum icon is now framed in a darker rectangle with a disclosure triangle: the track is now a Track Stack that contains one track for each microphone used to record the drum kit. Clicking the disclosure triangle displays the individual tracks and their channel strips. You will use Track Stacks in Lesson 5.

7   Click the Library button (or press Y) to close the Library window.

8   In Drum Kit Designer, click the snare.

This time the left pane displays a choice of many more snare drums (use your mouse to scroll down the list). The current snare, Black Brass, is selected.

9   Click another snare, and then click the Info button next to it.

A description of the selected snare opens.

Continue previewing different snares, and try listening to a verse or a chorus to hear your customized drum kit in action.

10   At the top of the left pane, click the Bell Brass snare.

11   In Drum Kit Designer, click the kick drum.

The info pop-up window updates to show you information on the selected kick drum.

Listen to the kick drum. This kick is the right choice for your song, but it has a long resonance. Typically, the faster the tempo of the song, the less resonance you want on the kick; otherwise, low frequencies build up and could become a problem during the mix. You may have seen drummers stuff an old blanket in their kick drum to dampen them. In Drum Kit Designer, you only have to raise the dampening level.

12 In the right pane, drag the Dampen knob up to about 75%, and click the kick to listen to it.

The kick's resonance is shortened.

You will now tune the toms, which are mainly used in the bridge section.

13 In the workspace, select the Bridge region.

14 In the Drummer Editor, click the Play button and mute the kick.

You can hear only the low and mid toms.

15 In Drum Kit Designer, click one of the toms.

The Edit panel opens with four tabs: All (for adjusting settings of all three toms in the kit together); and Low, Mid, and High (for adjusting settings of each individual tom).

16 Click the Mid tab and raise the Tune knob to around +155 cent.

You can hear the mid tom being pitched up as Kyle continues repeating the first half of the bridge.

If you want, feel free to continue exploring Drum Kit Designer and adjusting the sound of the hi-hat, ride, and crash cymbals.

17 In the Drummer editor, unmute the kick.

18 Stop playback and close the Drum Kit Designer window.

You have exchanged the snare for another one that sounds a little clearer, dampened the kick drum to tame its resonance, and tuned the mid tom to pitch it a bit higher. You have now fully customized both the drum performance and the drum kit.

Working with an Electronic Drummer

When drum machines first made their appearance in recording studios, drummers feared for their careers. The 1980s produced a number of hit songs in which live drummers were replaced by electronic drums programmed by music producers.

However, many producers quickly realized that to program exciting electronic drumbeats, they needed to develop the chops of a real drummer, whereas others simply chose to hire drummers for this task. In Logic, you can use Drummer to create virtual drum machine performances, turning beat creation into a fast and fun exercise.

Creating Hip Hop Beats

In this exercise, you will work with one of the Hip Hop drummers, adjusting its feel to control the human quality in the timing, and later you'll convert the Drummer region to a MIDI region to exercise complete control over each individual drum hit.

1   In the control bar, click the Library button, or press Y, to open the Library.

To make sure that the next drummer you choose brings along his own drum sound, you need to first verify that the padlock is no longer highlighted in the Sounds section of the Library.

2   Click the padlock to dim it.

3   In the Drummer section, choose Hip Hop > Maurice – Boom Bap.

In the inspector, the software instrument at the top of the Drummer track channel strip is Drum Machine Designer. The Drummer Editor updates to display drum machine samples. On the track, all the Drummer regions are refreshed to reflect Maurice's playing style.

4   Listen to a few sections.

Maurice plays a very loose, swung hip-hop groove. Your project tempo is still set to 142 bpm, but the drummer plays half time, so it sounds like 71 bpm. Let's work with the verse.

5   Drag the first Verse Arrangement marker to the ruler.

Cycle mode is on, and the cycle area corresponds to the Verse marker.

6   Select the Drummer region below the cycle area, and press Z to zoom in.

7   In the Drummer Editor, click the Details button.

When the "Auto half-time" checkbox is selected, the drummer automatically switches to half time when the project tempo is 110 bpm or faster; those fast tempos are rarely used in hip-hop.

8   Deselect "Auto half-time."

The drummer now plays at 142 bpm, which is much too fast for hip-hop.

9   In the LCD display, set the tempo to 87 bpm.

Maurice plays a very loose, almost sloppy beat. Let's tighten the performance.

10 Turn the Humanize knob all the way down.

The groove is now machine tight.

11 Turn the Swing knob up to 66%.

The drummer swings a little more, making the beat bouncier. Except for the fills at the end of the fourth and eighth bars in the region, it keeps repeating a fairly similar pattern. Let's make it vary the pattern a little more.

12 Turn the Phrase Variation knob all the way up.

Now the beat is slightly different in every bar.

Let's get rid of the crash cymbal on the first downbeat. Since the Drummer Editor doesn't give you complete control over every single drum hit, you need to convert the Drummer region to a MIDI region.

13 In the workspace, Control-click the selected Drummer region and choose Convert > Convert to MIDI Region.

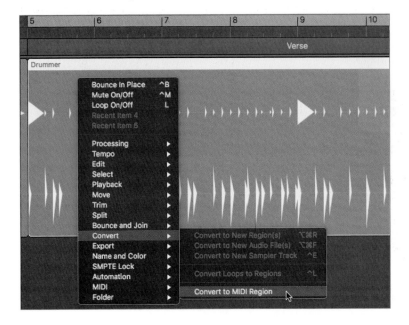

The yellow Drummer region is replaced by a green MIDI region that plays the same performance. The Drummer Editor is replaced by the Piano Roll Editor.

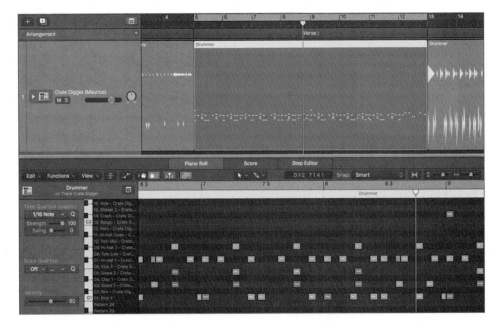

In the Piano Roll, the notes are represented by beams on a grid. The beams are positioned across a vertical piano keyboard that shows the MIDI note pitches. As long as your vertical zoom level is not too small, drum names are also displayed next to each key.

14 On the downbeat of bar 5, click the note representing the Crash cymbal (C#2).

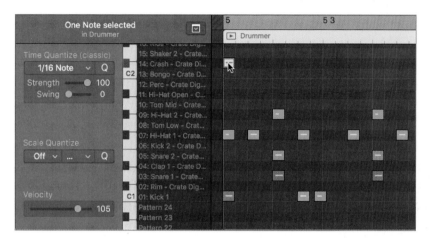

15 Press Delete to delete the selected note.

The crash cymbal is no longer triggered at the beginning of the verse.

You have replaced the acoustic drummer with an electronic drummer, adjusted the number of variations he plays, and made his playing sound tighter. Finally, you converted a Drummer region to a MIDI region to delete a single crash cymbal. In the next exercise, you'll explore the remaining parameters of the electronic Drummer Editor.

Creating an Electro-House Track

When you are working with Drum Machine Designer, the Drummer Editor allows you to restrict the complexity range of individual samples, making it possible to have, for example, a simple kick and snare beat while another sample follows a more complex pattern.

You will now switch drummers to create an electro-house drum track, and you'll create a ubiquitous four-on-the-floor kick and snare beat with a complex shaker pattern.

1 On the Drummer track, Control-click the MIDI region and choose Convert > Convert to Drummer Region.

In the Drummer region, the crash at the beginning of the region reappears. When you convert a MIDI region to a Drummer region, the region reverts to the Drummer performance you had before converting the region to MIDI.

2   In the Library, choose Electronic > Magnus – Big Room.

3   In the control bar, change the tempo to 132.

4   Listen to the verse.

You hear a rather straightforward dance groove. You will first work on the kick and snare beat.

5   In the Drummer Editor, click the Details button to go back to the basic view, and mute the shaker, hi-hat, and handclaps.

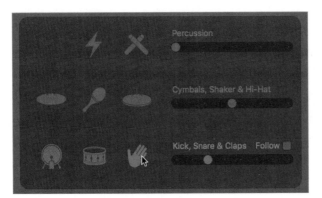

Only the kick and snare are playing. On the upper line in the Drummer region, a secondary kick plays every bar. Let's get rid of it.

6   In the XY pad, drag the puck to the left until the secondary kick disappears.

Now the snare may no longer play on beats 2 and 4 of every bar. You can fix that by adjusting its complexity range.

7   In the Drummer Editor, click the Details button.

You can drag the Complexity Range sliders for each individual drum piece to offset the complexity set by the puck in the XY pad.

8   Drag the snare's left Complexity Range slider toward the right until you hear the snare play on beats 2 and 4 of every bar.

Let's add a shaker to the party.

9   Click the shaker to unmute it.

The shaker plays a sixteenth note pattern, and it drops for a whole beat on beat 3 of bars 5, 7, 9, and 11. You are looking for a more consistent shaker groove.

10 Drag the shaker's left Complexity Range slider all the way to the right.

The shaker now plays the same sixteenth note pattern throughout the region.

After exploring the Complexity Range sliders, you now have a solid understanding of all the parameters in the Drummer Editor used by electronic drummers. It's now time to move on to the drum machine itself so you can customize the drum sounds.

Customizing the Drum Machine Sounds

Now that you're happy with the drummer performance, you can open Drum Machine Designer to adjust the mix, change the snare sample, tune it, and add some reverb.

1 At the top of the Big Room channel strip, click the Drum Machine Designer plug-in slot (DrmMchn).

The Drum Machine Designer interface opens.

The Drum Machine Designer interface consists of two parts:

▶ Drums cells (at the top) to select and trigger individual drum samples

▶ Smart Controls (at the bottom) to adjust various parameters

TIP ▶ To trigger Drum Machine Designer from your iPad, in Logic Remote tap the View menu and then tap Drum Pads. (You will learn how to use the Logic Remote app in Appendix A.)

2   In the Mix section, turn up the Perc & Shakrs knob.

The shaker sounds a little louder.

3   In the Effects section, try turning up the Pulse and turning down the High Cut Filter.

The Pulse knob controls a pulsating filter that affects the shaker pattern, whereas the High Cut Filter knob muffles the entire kit.

TIP ▶ To determine which plug-in a knob controls, Control-click the knob and choose Open Plug-in Window.

4   Click the buttons next to the Pulse and High Cut Filter knobs.

Both effects are turned off, and you can hear the full frequency range of the drum sounds.

NOTE ▶ You will learn how to record knob movements in Lesson 10.

5   At the upper right of the Smart Controls, click the Sends button.

The Smart Controls display knobs that control the amount of delay and reverb for different drum kit elements.

6   In the Group Reverb section, turn Snare & Claps all the way up.

You can hear a short reverb added to the snare; however, that's not the type of reverb sound you're after. You will later find a more suitable reverb for this snare, so let's turn that one down.

7   Turn Snare & Claps all the way down.

You will now swap the kit piece patch for the Snare.

8 Click the Snare 1 cell.

The Snare 1 cell is selected, the sound for that cell plays, and the Smart Controls update to display knobs affecting that cell.

> **TIP** At the top of Drum Machine Designer, click the drum machine icon or patch name to return to the main Smart Controls for this preset.

9 In the Snare 1 cell, click the S button.

The snare is soloed.

10 Open the Library.

11 In the Sounds section, choose Snares > Snare 2 – Analog Circuits.

You hear the snare you just selected. In Drum Machine Designer, the cell displays the new patch name.

> **TIP** To use a sample that is not in the Logic library, drag the sample onto the desired Drum Machine Designer cell.

12 In the Smart Controls, turn the Pitch knob down to A2.

13 Turn the Length knob down to shorten the snare sound.

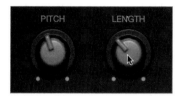

In the inspector, the right channel strip controls the sound of the selected cell in Drum Machine Designer. Let's add the desired reverb to the snare.

14 On the right channel strip in the inspector, click the first empty Audio FX insert, and choose Reverb > ChromaVerb.

15 In the ChromaVerb window, from the Settings pop-up menu, choose Rooms > Punchy Room.

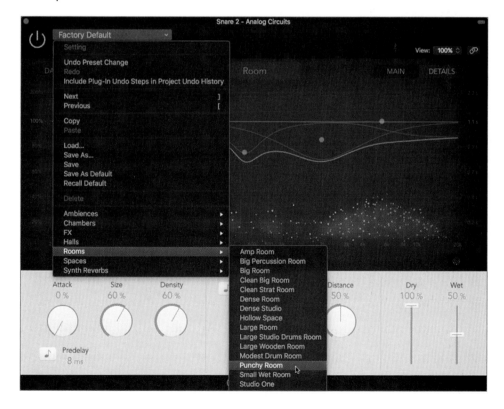

16 In ChromaVerb, drag the Wet slider up to increase the amount of reverb.

17 In Drum Machine Designer, click the S button in the Snare 2 cell to turn solo off.

You have adjusted the kit mix, played with some main effects, swapped one of the drum samples, adjusted its sound, and added a plug-in to its channel strip to get the sound you wanted.

You have produced drums for a whole song, and you've learned many ways to edit the drummer's performance and change the feel. You also customized drum kits to get your desired sound. With Drummer, Drum Kit Designer, and Drum Machine Designer, Logic Pro X allows you to quickly lay down a rhythmic foundation for a wide range of modern music genres.

Lesson Review

1. How do you choose a drummer?
2. How do you choose a new drummer while keeping the current drum kit?
3. Where do you edit Drummer regions?
4. How do you mute or unmute drum parts?
5. How do you make the drummer play softer or louder, simpler or more complex?
6. How do you access the Feel knob to make the drummer play behind or ahead of the beat?
7. How do you open Smart Controls?
8. How do you open Drum Kit Designer or Drum Machine Designer?
9. When customizing an acoustic drum kit, how can you access all the available drum kit pieces?

10. How do you dampen or tune an individual drum on an acoustic drum kit?

11. How do you convert a Drummer region to a MIDI region?

12. How do you swap samples in Drum Machine Designer?

13. How can you use audio effect plug-ins for an individual cell in Drum Machine Designer?

Answers

1. Ensure that a Drummer track is selected. Open the Library, and in the Drummer section, choose a category and a drummer.

2. In the Library, click the padlock icon in the Sounds section.

3. In the Drummer Editor at the bottom of the main window

4. Click the drum parts in the drum kit that is displayed in the Drummer Editor.

5. Move the puck on the XY pad.

6. Click the Details button at the bottom right of the Drummer Editor.

7. Click the Smart Controls button in the control bar, or press B.

8. Click the icon at the top of the Library, or click the software instrument plug-in slot at the top of the channel strip.

9. Select the appropriate Producer Kit in the Library.

10. In Drum Kit Designer, click a drum and adjust the settings in the Edit panel.

11. Control-click the region, and choose Convert > Convert to MIDI Region.

12. Click a cell and choose a new sample in the Library.

13. Click a cell and insert your plug-in on the right channel strip in the inspector.

Keyboard Shortcuts

Main Window

B	Opens the Smart Controls
G	Opens the global tracks
Command-Shift-N	Opens a new file without opening the Templates dialog
Y	Opens the Library

5

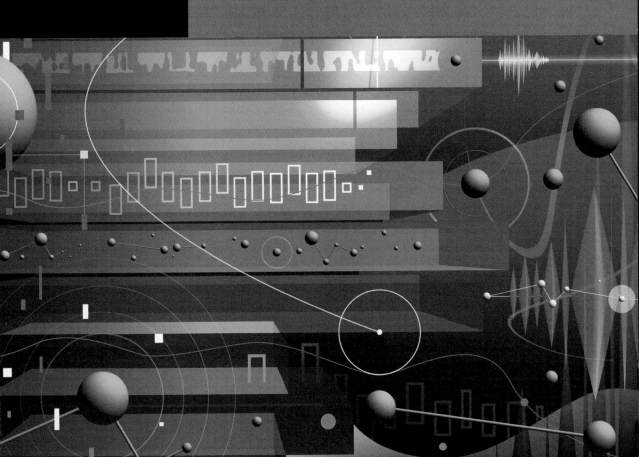

Using Patches and Recording MIDI

MIDI (Musical Instrument Digital Interface) was created in 1983 to standardize the way electronic musical instruments communicate. Today, MIDI is extensively used throughout the music industry to record and program synthesizers and samplers. Many TV and film composers use MIDI to sequence large software sound libraries, getting ever closer to realizing the sound of a real orchestra.

MIDI sequences can be compared to piano rolls, the perforated paper rolls once used by mechanical player pianos. Like the punched holes in piano rolls, MIDI events do not contain audio. They contain note information such as pitch and velocity. To turn MIDI data into sound, MIDI events are routed to a software instrument or to an external MIDI instrument.

There are two basic types of MIDI events: MIDI note events, which trigger musical notes, and MIDI continuous controller (MIDI CC) events, which control parameters such as volume, pan, or pitch bend.

For example, when you press C3 on a MIDI controller keyboard, the keyboard sends a "note on" MIDI event. The note on event contains the pitch of the note (C3) and the velocity of the note (which indicates how fast the key was struck, thereby showing how hard the musician pressed the key).

By connecting a MIDI controller keyboard to Logic, you can use Logic to route the MIDI events to a virtual software instrument or to an external MIDI instrument. The instrument reacts to the note on event by producing a C3 note, and the velocity typically determines how loud the note sounds.

When a MIDI controller keyboard is connected to your computer, and its driver is properly installed (some devices are class-compliant and don't require a driver installation), you can use that keyboard to record MIDI in Logic. Logic automatically routes all incoming MIDI events to the record-enabled software instrument or external MIDI track.

> **NOTE** ▶ When connecting certain MIDI controllers, Logic opens a dialog asking if you want to automatically assign its controls. To follow the exercises in this lesson, click No. If you've clicked Auto Assign before in this dialog, choose Logic Pro X > Control Surfaces > Preferences, click the MIDI Controllers tab, and deselect the Auto checkbox for all listed controllers.

> **TIP** ▶ If you don't have a MIDI controller keyboard, choose Window > Show Musical Typing (or press Command-K) to turn your Mac keyboard into a polyphonic MIDI controller. Pressing the Z and X keys allows you to choose the octave range, and pressing C and V lets you adjust the note velocities. Keep in mind that you may need to close the Musical Typing window (or press Command-K) to access some of the Logic key commands.

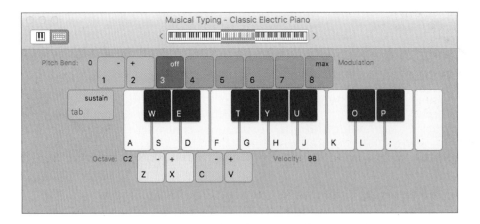

TIP ▶ You will apply the Logic Remote app to use your iPad as a wireless MIDI controller in Appendix A, "Controlling Logic with an iPad Using Logic Remote."

Using a Patch from the Library

When working with software instruments in Logic, the MIDI events can be recorded, created, and edited inside MIDI regions placed on the track. The MIDI events generated by playing your MIDI keyboard are routed to the record-enabled track in the Tracks area. From the track, those real-time events from your keyboard, or the events played back from MIDI regions on the tracks, are routed to the top of the channel strip. They can be preprocessed by MIDI effect plug-ins before the MIDI data is passed to the instrument plug-in. The instrument produces an audio signal that can be further processed using audio effect plug-ins. The audio can then be adjusted with the Volume fader and Pan knob before being routed to the output destination.

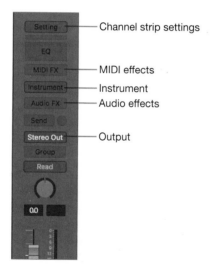

The Setting button at the top of a channel strip allows you to load or save channel strip settings, which contain all the plug-ins inserted on a channel strip and their individual settings.

The Library lets you load or save patches, channel strip settings, or plug-in settings. A patch can be a single channel strip setting, or multiple channel strips and their channel strip settings.

TIP ▶ To see a plug-in's settings in the Library, click to the left of the plug-in on the channel strip in the inspector. A blue triangle and a white frame indicate which plug-in's settings the Library is currently displaying.

In this exercise, you will create a software instrument track, choose a patch from the Library, and examine the channel strips created in the Mixer.

1   Choose File > New (or press Command-Shift-N).

If a project was already open, an alert asks if you want to close the current project. Click Close (a Save dialog then prompts you to save it).

2   In the New Track dialog, click Software Instrument. From the Instrument pop-up menu, choose Empty Channel Strip, and make sure all checkboxes are deselected. Click Create.

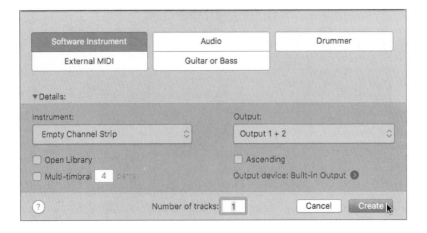

A new, empty software instrument track is created.

3   In the control bar, click the Mixer button (or press X).

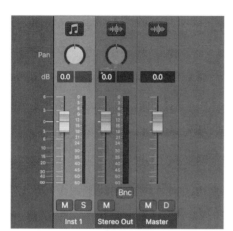

The Mixer opens and shows three channel strips that are, from left to right:

▶   The software instrument channel strip you just created (Inst 1)

▶   The Stereo Out channel strip

▶   The Master channel strip

You will now load a patch for the selected software instrument track while watching what happens in the Mixer.

4   In the control bar, click the Library button (or press Y).

The Library opens to the left of the inspector.

5   In the Library, choose Piano > Steinway Grand Piano.

TIP ▶   In the Library, you can press the Up and Down Arrow keys to select categories or patches in a list, and press the Left and Right Arrow keys to navigate to the left and right columns.

6   Play a few keys on your MIDI keyboard to hear the piano sound.

7   In the Mixer, look at the channel strips.

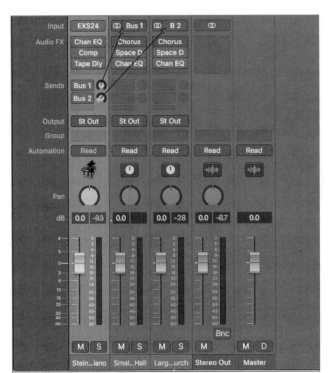

On the software instrument channel strip (Steinway Grand Piano), a channel strip setting is loaded, containing an EXS24 (the Logic sampler) instrument plug-in and three audio effect plug-ins: a Channel EQ, a Compressor, and a Tape Delay.

Two new auxiliary channel strips are also created (Small Hall/1.3s Diffuse Hall and Large Hall/6.6s Botta Church), each one with its own channel strip setting. The software instrument channel strip has two bus sends that route the audio signal to the inputs of the two auxiliaries, set to Bus 1 and Bus 2 (B 2). Together, the software instrument channel strip setting, along with the two auxiliaries and their channel strip settings, make up the Steinway Grand Piano patch.

In a Mixer, a bus transports the audio signal from one channel strip to another. Here, Bus 1 and Bus 2 route the stereo audio signal of the piano to two different reverberation effects on the two auxiliaries.

TIP ▶ In Logic, a single bus can transport a mono, stereo, or surround audio signal.

8   On the Steinway Piano channel strip, next to the Bus 1 send, drag the bus Send Level knob all the way up.

Play the piano with your MIDI keyboard. You can hear the reverberation sound of a smaller room.

9   Next to the Bus 1 send, lower the Send Level knob all the way down.

The piano now has a small amount of reverb that comes from the Bus 2 send.

10   Next to the Bus 2 send, lower the send level all the way down.

The piano now sounds completely dry with no reverberation.

11   Next to the Bus 2 send, raise the send level all the way up.

You can hear the reverb of the second auxiliary, which sounds like a much bigger room. Notice that this reverb sustains for a longer time than the first one.

12   Continue adjusting the bus send levels to compare the sound of the two reverbs, and then set them to a level that sounds good to you.

> **TIP**   To load a patch without its bus sends and auxiliary channel strips, start with an empty software instrument channel strip. At the lower left of the Library, from the Action menu, choose Enable Patch Merging. Then deselect the Sends button.

13   Close the Mixer.

Now that you know how to choose a patch from the Library, and how to adjust the amount of reverb using the bus Send Level knobs, you will create and save your own custom patch.

Creating a Layered Sound Patch

Well before recording was invented, composers used instrumental sound layering to thicken sounds. In a classical orchestra, you often hear multiple musicians playing the same part at the same time. When all the violins play a melody together, you hear a rich warm tone and the emotional level is raised.

Sound layering is a common technique used by music producers to make just about any instrument sound thicker, or to mix the timbres of different sounds. For example, many vocals on commercial songs are doubled (that is, the singer records two identical performances that are played back simultaneously), and dance music producers often layer multiple kick drum samples, such as combining a kick drum with a strong percussive attack and another that has a boomy sustain.

In Logic, Track Stacks allow you to combine a group of tracks and control them as a single track. Track Stacks can be used to organize tracks you want to group together (such as drum tracks or backup vocal tracks). They can also be used to group software instrument tracks, so that the MIDI notes on a single track can trigger all of the instruments in the Track Stack.

In this exercise, you will create a Track Stack for two different synthesizer patches and save the Track Stack as a new patch.

1   Choose File > New (or press Command-Shift-N), and when prompted, close but don't save the existing project.

2   In the New Tracks dialog, choose Software Instrument. Set "Number of tracks" to 2, and click Create.

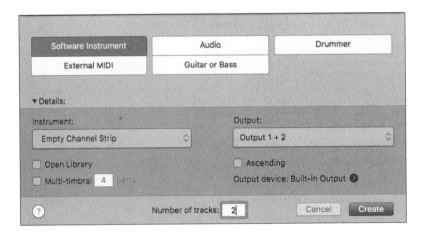

Two empty software instrument tracks are created.

3 Click the Library button (or press Y) to open the Library.

4 In the Tracks area, select the first track, and in the Library, choose Synthesizer > Lead > Nightlife Lead.

5 Play your MIDI keyboard.

The synth sounds modern; it is quite edgy and buzzy. Try playing a bass line in the C1–C2 range. This modern bass has a lot of character, but it lacks the body and thickness of an older analog synth.

6 In the Tracks area, select track 2, and in the Library, choose Synthesizer > Lead > 70s Analog Lead.

That synth is more rounded and warm. Plus, it has more low frequencies, which will bring body to the layered sound. Let's select both tracks and create a Track Stack for them.

TIP ▶ To hear both sounds layered before you create the Track Stack, record-enable both track headers and play your MIDI keyboard.

7 Shift-click the unselected track header to select both track headers.

8 Choose Track > Create Track Stack (or press Command-Shift-D).

A dialog lets you choose between a folder stack or a summing stack. To group software instruments and work with the MIDI data on the main track of a Track Stack, you must use a summing stack.

9 Choose Summing Stack, and click Create.

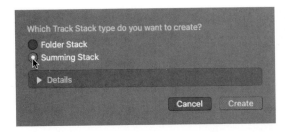

In the Tracks area, the main track of the new summing stack appears at the top, and the two original software instrument tracks become subtracks of the Track Stack.

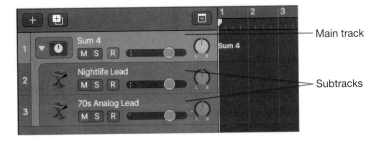

In the workspace, the main track and the subtracks have a green background to indicate that they all belong to a summing stack.

10 Make sure the main track of the Track Stack is record-enabled, and play your MIDI keyboard.

You can now hear the layered sound combining both the Nightlife Lead and the 70s Analog Lead patches.

11 Try muting either subtrack inside the Track Stack.

Muting a subtrack allows you to determine exactly what each subtrack adds to the layered sound. When you mute Nightlife Lead, the sound loses its edge and buzzy quality. When you mute 70s Analog Lead, the sound loses body and warmth.

12 Unmute both subtracks.

Let's assign the main track an icon that will be saved along with the patch.

13 On the main track, Control-click the icon, and choose a keyboard icon.

14 At the bottom of the Library, click Save.

15 In the Save dialog, type a filename for the patch, such as *Thick Bass*, and save it to the default location.

In the Library, a new User Patches category is created in the left column and your new patch is selected inside it.

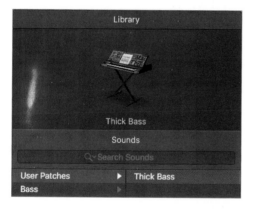

In the workspace, the main track in the Track Stack is renamed after the patch you saved.

16 On the Track Stack's main track header, click the disclosure triangle next to the icon.

The Track Stack is now closed and appears as a single track. It retains all functionality, and as long as the Track Stack is record-enabled, you can continue playing or recording the layered patch from your MIDI keyboard.

Now that you have saved your custom patch in the Library, it will be available in any project you open in Logic whenever a track of the same type (a software instrument track) is selected. Selecting the Thick Bass patch from the Library will replace the selected software instrument track with the summing stack and its two subtracks.

Mapping Controller Knobs to Plug-in Parameters

In Lesson 4, you used Smart Controls as a one-stop shop for adjusting multiple parameters, such as a bus send level, parameters of the instrument plug-in, and parameters of the channel EQ plug-in.

This time you will map a Smart Control knob to a plug-in parameter, and assign a real knob or fader on your MIDI controller to that Smart Control knob. Finally, you'll save your custom Smart Control layout within the patch.

Opening the Plug-Ins for Mapping

In this exercise, you'll select a patch in the Library and open the plug-in you want to control. In the Smart Controls pane, you will map one of that plug-in's knobs to a screen control.

1 Drag the track header of the main track into the inspector to delete the track.

The New Track dialog opens.

2 Create one new software instrument track.

3 Open the Library, and select Synthesizer > Bass > Dirty Fifth.

4 Play your MIDI keyboard.

The synth sounds thick and gritty. Wouldn't it be fun to make its timbre evolve while you play some notes? To do so, you will first open the plug-in windows that have parameters you can map to screen controls.

5   In the inspector, click in the middle of the Ringshifter plug-in slot to open the plug-in.

The Ringshifter plug-in window opens.

TIP If the presence of plug-in windows hinders your ability to interact with the main window, press V to toggle all plug-in windows on and off.

TIP ▶ To resize a plug-in window, drag its lower-right corner or use the View pop-up menu in the plug-in header.

Mapping Screen Controls to Parameters

Now that you have opened the Ringshifter plug-in, you can use the Smart Controls pane to map a screen control to the Ringshifter's Frequency knob.

1   In the control bar, click the Smart Controls button (or press B).

The Smart Controls pane opens at the bottom of the main window, displaying a collection of preassigned screen control knobs and buttons.

2   At the upper left of the Smart Controls pane, click the Inspector button.

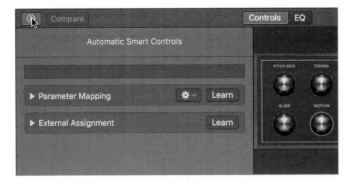

The Smart Controls inspector opens. It shows the parameter assignments for the selected screen control. You will map only one screen control knob, so let's choose a simpler layout.

3   At the top of the Smart Controls inspector, click the layout name, and choose Factory
    Layouts > Soundscape 6.

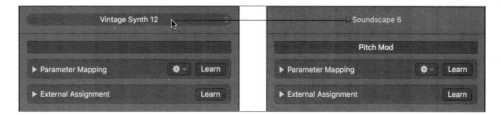

The simpler Soundscape 6 layout appears. It has only six knobs. The first (labeled
Pitch Mod) is highlighted in blue to indicate that it is selected. First let's remove all
factory mappings for this patch.

4   In the Parameter Mapping area, from the action menu, choose Delete all Patch
    Mappings.

All screen controls for the current patch are unmapped.

You now will map the first screen controls knob so that it controls the big Frequency
knob in the Ringshifter plug-in.

5   In the Parameter Mapping area, click the Learn button.

The first screen control knob is highlighted in red, indicating that it is ready to be mapped.

6   In the Ringshifter, click the big Frequency knob.

In the Smart Controls pane, the highlighted screen control is renamed "Frequency."

7   In the Parameter Mapping area, click the Learn button to turn off Learn mode.

8   Close the Smart Controls inspector.

In the Smart Controls pane, the mapped Frequency knob is displayed, and the unmapped knobs are hidden.

9   In the Smart Controls pane, drag the Frequency knob up and down while you play a few notes on your keyboard.

The big Frequency knob in the Ringshifter moves along with the Smart Control knob, and you can hear the Ringshifter effect modulate your synth sound.

10   Close the Ringshifter plug-in window.

You can now save this patch along with your custom Smart Control layout and mappings.

11   At the bottom of the Library, click the Save button.

12   In the Save dialog, name your patch *Dirty Fifth Shifter*, and click Save.

You have created and saved your own Smart Control layout, with a screen control mapped to a plug-in parameter. Smart Controls allow you to unite all the controls you need in a single pane, which makes it easy to control multiple parameters in multiple plug-ins without opening the plug-in windows.

Assigning MIDI Controller Knobs to Screen Controls

As fun as it is to tweak the frequency of the Ringshifter while playing on your keyboard, it's not usually practical to have one hand on the mouse tweaking a knob on your computer screen while the other is playing the keyboard. However, most recent MIDI keyboards and MIDI control surfaces have knobs or faders that can send MIDI Continuous Controller data to Logic, so let's assign a hardware knob to the screen control in the Smart Controls pane.

1   Open the Smart Controls inspector.

2   In the External Assignment area, click the Learn button.

NOTE ▶ When the External Assignment Learn button is on, do not play notes on your keyboard, or touch knobs, faders, or wheels other than the one you intend to assign to the selected onscreen controller. If you do, that unintended action will also be learned as an assignment and may lead to unexpected results.

3   On your MIDI keyboard, turn a knob. Don't be timid. Move the knob all the way down and all the way up, if necessary. When the knob is assigned, it adjusts the Frequency screen control in the Smart Controls pane (which in turns controls the Ringshifter plug-in's Frequency parameter).

4   In the External Assignment area, click the Learn button to turn it off.

5   Close the Smart Controls inspector.

6   On your MIDI keyboard, play keys while turning the assigned knob.

As you move the knob on your keyboard, the Frequency screen control moves in the Smart Controls pane, and you can hear the Ringshifter effect process the sound.

7   Choose File > Close Project, but do not save the project.

You have assigned a physical knob on your MIDI controller keyboard to the first screen control in the Smart Controls pane of any patch you load. Being able to control Logic's sound effects remotely from your MIDI Controller allows you to place all of your focus on your musical performance.

Using the Arpeggiator MIDI Plug-In

MIDI effects are plug-ins that can process the MIDI data within a track before it reaches the instrument plug-in, regardless of whether it was generated in real time using your MIDI keyboard or placed in the MIDI regions on the track during playback. A MIDI plug-in may change the pitch and velocity of notes or even create new MIDI note or controller events.

In this exercise, you will hold down a chord on your MIDI keyboard and process the chord using the Arpeggiator MIDI plug-in, which automatically arpeggiates a chord's notes while staying in sync with the project.

1   Go to Logic Pro X > Lessons and open **05 Dub Beat**. This project has two empty software instrument tracks (Inst 1 and Low Down Dub).

2   On the first track, double-click the Inst 1 name, and rename the track *Synth*.

3   On the Synth channel strip, click the Instrument slot, and choose Retro Synth.

The Retro Synth plug-in opens. This modeling instrument can imitate a wide range of classic synths and their specific synthesis techniques. In the Oscillator section at the upper left, four tabs let you access one of the four synthesizer engines: analog modeling (ANALOG), synchronized oscillators (SYNC), wavetable synthesis (TABLE), and frequency modulation (FM).

4   Play a few notes on your keyboard.

You can hear the Retro Synth play a classic analog synth sound.

TIP ▶ To hear the results of your actions, continue playing your MIDI keyboard as you make adjustments throughout this lesson.

5   In the inspector on the Synth channel strip, click the MIDI FX slot, and choose Arpeggiator.

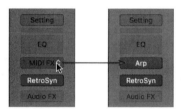

The Arpeggiator opens.

6   Hold down a single note. The Arpeggiator starts repeating it every sixteenth note.

7   Hold down a chord. The Arpeggiator plays one note at a time every sixteenth note, from the lowest note to the highest one.

8   Press the Spacebar.

You can hear the Low Down Dub beat on track 2. Track 2 uses the Ultrabeat instrument plug-in, which has a built-in sequencer. This is why you can hear the instrument play a beat even though you don't see any MIDI regions on its track.

For the rest of this exercise, feel free to stop and resume playback when you need a break, or when you want to focus on the arpeggiated synth.

9   At the top of the Arpeggiator, click Latch.

When Latch is enabled, the Arpeggiator memorizes the last chord you played as long as the project continues playing. You can click the Play button at the upper left of the Arpeggiator to stop and start playback.

10 Play a chord and release the keys. The arpeggio continues to play.

11 Play another chord to hear the arpeggiated chord.

Next to the Latch button, notice that Mode is set to Transpose. In that mode, you can use your MIDI keyboard to transpose the arpeggio to a different key.

12 Play a single key on your keyboard.

The previous chord is transposed, so it starts on the pitch of the note you play.

13 In the Note Order section, click the Down button.

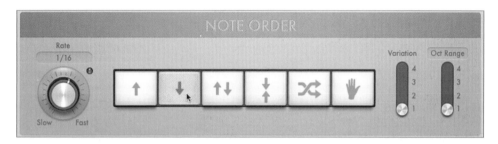

The arpeggio now plays from the highest note to the lowest note.

14 Drag the Oct Range switch to position 3.

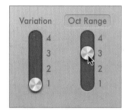

The Arpeggiator repeats over a three-octave range.

15 In Retro Synth, at the lower right, try playing with the amplifier envelope (AMP ENV) by dragging the handles on the display or by adjusting the four parameters around the display: A, D, S, R (for Attack, Decay, Sustain, Release). Try making the sound of the synth evolve from long envelopes to very short ones.

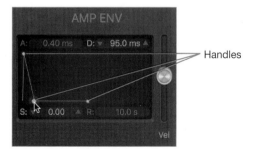

Handles

16 In the Arpeggiator, try adjusting the Rate knob to change how fast the chord is arpeggiated.

Keep in mind that shorter amp envelopes work best for faster rates.

17 Choose File > Close Project, but do not save your project.

The Arpeggiator MIDI plug-in processes a simple chord played on your keyboard into simple and complex arpeggios. You've learned how to choose different note orders and their variations, and to expand the arpeggio over multiple octaves. You also manipulated the synthesizer's filter and amp envelopes to make the sound evolve while the arpeggio is playing.

MIDI plug-ins give you more tools to process MIDI events in real time. Feel free to continue exploring the possibilities, perhaps by choosing different instruments to arpeggiate.

Recording MIDI

In Logic, the basic techniques used to record MIDI are similar to the techniques you used to record audio in Lesson 2. You will now observe the MIDI In display in the control bar as you send MIDI events to Logic and record a simple piano part.

1 Choose File > New (or press Command-Shift-N).

2 In the New Tracks dialog, choose Software Instrument. Make sure the Instrument pop-up menu is set to Empty Channel Strip, and click Create.

3 In the Control bar, click the Library button (or press Y).

4 In the Library, choose Piano > Steinway Grand Piano.

5 Play a few notes on your MIDI keyboard while observing the LCD display.

MIDI input activity

A small dot appears at the upper right of the LCD display to indicate that Logic is receiving MIDI events. These small dots can be useful to quickly troubleshoot MIDI connections.

NOTE ▸ When Logic sends MIDI events to external MIDI devices, a small dot appears at the lower right of the LCD display.

6   Play a chord on your MIDI keyboard.

The MIDI input activity monitor displays the chord name.

Logic can provide a more detailed view of the incoming MIDI events.

7   To the right of the LCD display, click the small arrow, and choose Custom.

The Custom LCD display appears, with a MIDI input activity monitor that shows incoming MIDI events in more detail.

8   Hold down a key on your MIDI keyboard.

A note icon indicates that the event received is a MIDI note on event. You can also see the MIDI channel number of the MIDI event, the note's pitch, and its velocity. In the previous image, the event's MIDI channel is 1, its pitch is D2, and its velocity is 98.

NOTE ▸ MIDI events can be sent on up to 16 different MIDI channels, which allows you to control different timbres on different channels when using multi-timbral instruments.

9   Release the key on your MIDI keyboard.

Depending on your controller, in the LCD display you may see a note on event with a velocity of zero, or you may see a note with a strike through it, which represents a note off event.

NOTE ▶ Pressing and releasing a key on a MIDI keyboard sends two events: a note on event and a note off event. However, most MIDI editors represent the two events as a single note event with a length attribute.

You could start recording a piano part now, but first let's open the Piano Roll so you can watch the MIDI notes appear on the grid as they are recorded.

10 In the control bar, click the Editors button, and at the top of the Editors pane, ensure that Piano Roll is selected (or press P).

The Piano Roll opens at the bottom of the main window.

11 Make sure the playhead is at the beginning of the project, and click the Record button (or press R).

The LCD display and the playhead turn red to indicate that Logic is recording. The playhead jumps back one bar, giving you a four-beat count-in, and you can hear the metronome.

12 When the playhead appears, play quarter notes for a couple of bars to record a very simple bass line.

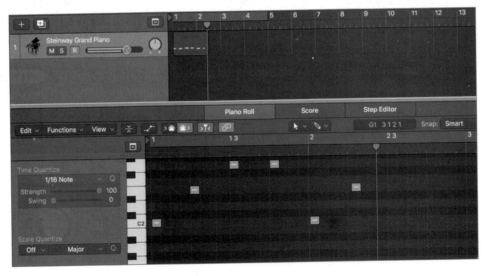

When you play the first note, a red MIDI region appears on the record-enabled track. The region's length constantly updates to include the most recent MIDI event received.

The MIDI notes appear in the Piano Roll and on the region in the workspace as you record them.

NOTE ▸ If the pitch of the notes you record is outside the range of pitches displayed in the Piano Roll, you will not see the notes as they are recorded.

13 Stop recording.

The region is now shaded green. It is named *Steinway Grand Piano.* You can see the recorded notes in the Piano Roll.

TIP ▸ To see all the notes in the Piano Roll, make sure they are all deselected and press Z.

14 In the Piano Roll, click the Play button at the upper left of the region.

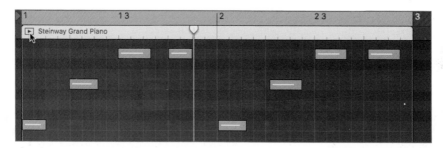

The region starts playback in Solo and Cycle modes. If you are not happy with your performance, you can undo it (Command-Z) and try again.

If you are mostly happy but one or two notes need correction, you can quickly fix them in the Piano Roll:

▸   Drag a note vertically to change its pitch.

▸   Drag a note horizontally to change its timing.

▸   Click a note, and press Delete to remove it.

You will learn how to edit MIDI events in more detail in Lesson 6.

15 Click the region's Play button again (or press the Spacebar) to stop playback.

Solo and Cycle modes are both turned off.

Correcting the Timing of a MIDI Recording

If you are not happy with the timing of your MIDI performance, you can correct the timing of the notes using a time-correction method called *quantization*. To quantize a MIDI region, you choose a note value from the Quantize menu in the Region inspector, and inside the region, the notes snap to the nearest absolute value.

Quantizing MIDI Regions

In this exercise, you will quantize the piano passage you recorded in the previous exercise so that the notes are in sync with the metronome.

> **NOTE ▶** If you were quite happy with the timing of your performance, you may want to undo your previous recording and record again with a less accurate timing so that you can more clearly hear the benefits of quantization.

1 In the workspace, make sure the piano region is still selected.

2 In the Region inspector, click the Quantize value (currently set to off) and choose 1/4 Note while looking at the notes in the Piano Roll.

All the MIDI notes in the piano region snap to the nearest quarter note.

3 In the control bar, click the Metronome button (or press K) to turn it on.

4 Play the piano region. The notes are now perfectly in sync with the metronome.

In Logic, quantizing is a nondestructive operation. You can always revert the notes to their original position.

5 In the Region inspector, set Quantize to off.

In the Piano Roll, the notes return to their original recording positions.

6 In the Region inspector, set Quantize back to 1/4 Note.

The notes are once more in sync with the metronome.

7 Turn off the metronome, and stop playback.

Choosing Default Quantization Settings

You can choose a default MIDI quantization setting so that any new MIDI recording is automatically quantized to that value. This is very useful when you are not completely confident of your timing chops. Because the Quantize setting is nondestructive, you can always adjust it or turn it off for that region after you're finished recording.

1 In the workspace, click the background.

All regions are deselected, and the Region inspector now displays the MIDI Defaults parameters. The MIDI Defaults settings will be automatically applied to any new MIDI region you record.

2 In the MIDI Defaults parameters, set Quantize to 1/8 Note.

3 In the workspace, click the piano region, and press Delete to delete the region.

4 Move the playhead to the beginning of the project, and click the Record button (or press R).

Record another simple bass line, as you did in the previous exercise. Feel free to play eighth notes this time, since that's the Quantize value you selected.

5   Stop recording.

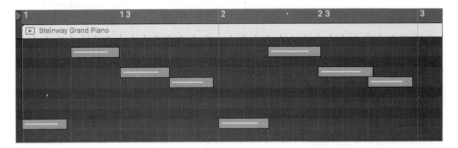

In the Piano Roll, the notes immediately snap to the nearest eighth note on the grid. In the Region inspector, the Quantize parameter for the new piano region is set to 1/8 Note. Remember that the Quantize setting is nondestructive, which means that you can still turn it off.

6   In the Region inspector, set Quantize to off. In the Piano Roll, the notes move to their original recorded positions.

7   Set Quantize back to 1/8 Note.

Merging Recordings into a MIDI Region

Sometimes you may want to record a MIDI performance in several passes. For example, when recording piano, you want to record just the left hand, and then record the right hand in a second pass. Or you could record drums in multiple passes, recording the kick drum first, then the snare drum, then the hi-hat, then the crash cymbal, building up a drum beat by focusing on a single piece of the drum kit at a time.

In Logic, when recording MIDI events on top of an existing MIDI region, you can choose to merge the new recording with the existing MIDI region.

Recording into an Existing MIDI Region

In the previous exercise, you recorded a simple bass line onto a piano track. Now you will record chords as you listen to your bass line, merging the new chords with that bass line inside the same MIDI region. First, you will choose the correct recording setting to merge your new recording with the existing region.

1   Make sure Record > Overlapping MIDI Recordings > Cycle Off > Merge is chosen.

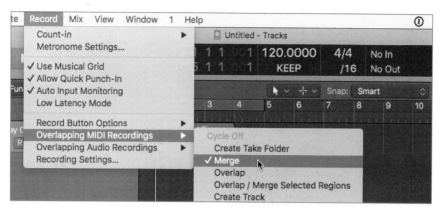

From now on the new recordings will be merged with the existing region on the track.

2   Move the playhead to the beginning and start recording.

This time, play only a couple of chords that complement the bass line you previously recorded.

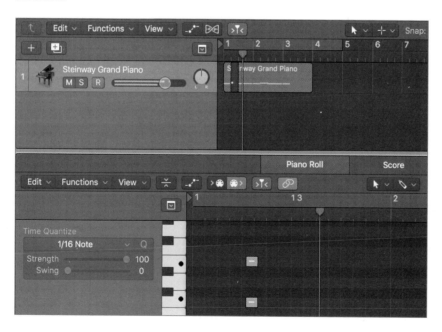

3   Stop recording.

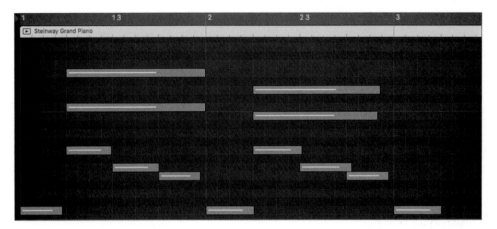

The new notes immediately snap to the nearest eighth note on the grid. On the track, the *Steinway Grand Piano* MIDI region contains all the notes recorded in this exercise and the previous one.

TIP ▸ You can also use this technique to add MIDI controller events such as pitch bend or modulation to a region after you have recorded the MIDI notes.

Merging Recordings in Cycle Mode

Recording MIDI in Cycle mode allows you to continuously repeat the same section and record new events only when you are ready. This can be very useful when recording a drum pattern. You can loop over a section, building up the drum groove by adding new elements during each pass of the cycle while listening to the drums you have already recorded.

When you are recording MIDI in Cycle mode, notes recorded in all consecutive passes of the cycle are merged into a single MIDI region. In this exercise, you will record drums in Cycle mode, first recording the kick, then the snare, and finally the hi-hat.

First, let's close the current project and create a new one.

1   Choose File > Close Project (or press Command-Option-W), and when prompted, close but don't save the existing project.

TIP ► When only one window is open in Logic, you can close the project by choosing File > Close (or pressing Command-W).

2   Choose File > New. In the New Tracks dialog, make sure Software Instrument is selected, and click Create.

In a new project, the menu option Record > Overlapping MIDI Recording > Cycle On > Merge is selected by default. Recording in Cycle mode will place all recorded notes in the same region, which is the desired behavior for this exercise.

3   In the control bar, click the Library button (or press Y).

4   In the Library, select Drum Kit > Brooklyn.

The Brooklyn patch is loaded, including a channel strip setting that is loaded for the software instrument channel strip in the inspector. It consists of the Drum Kit Designer instrument plug-in, and the Channel EQ, Compressor, and Multipressor audio effect plug-ins. The channel strip sends to bus 1, and if you open the Mixer, you can see a new auxiliary—and its plug-ins—with its input set to bus 1.

Let's customize the LCD display so that you can see the detailed MIDI input activity monitor.

5   To the right of the LCD display, click the small arrow, and choose Custom.

Before you start recording, you need to locate the keys that trigger the kick, snare, and hi-hat on your MIDI controller. You will use:

▶   C1: kick

▶   D1: snare

▶   F#1: closed hi-hat

▶   A#1: open hi-hat

6 Play the lowest C key on your MIDI keyboard while watching the MIDI activity in the LCD display.

If the display doesn't show a C1, you can use the Octave –/+ buttons on your keyboard to offset the pitch range. Once you've found C1, locate D1 (the next white key to the right), F#1, and A#1 (respectively the first and the last keys of the next group of three black keys to the right).

7 In the upper half of the ruler, click the cycle area to turn on Cycle mode.

Since you don't have a region in the workspace, the Region inspector displays the MIDI Defaults settings.

8 In the Region inspector, set Quantize to 1/16 Note.

You will now record the drums one at a time. Let's open the Piano Roll to see the notes appear on the grid as you record them.

9 In the control bar, click the Editors button (or press P) to open the Piano Roll.

10 Start recording. You hear a four-beat count-in before the playhead reaches the beginning of the cycle area.

11 Play C1 notes on the first and third beat of every bar.

When the playhead reaches the end of the cycle, it jumps back and starts a new pass. You can hear the kick drum notes that you just recorded. Notice that the notes snap to the nearest sixteenth note because you chose that value as your MIDI Defaults Quantize setting.

You have all the time in the world before you continue to record. As long as you don't play anything, Logic continues cycling over the existing region, playing back your kick drums. And if you forgot to play one or two kick drum notes, you can record them during one of the subsequent cycle passes.

12 Play D1 notes on the second and fourth beat of every bar. The kick and the snare should alternate on every beat.

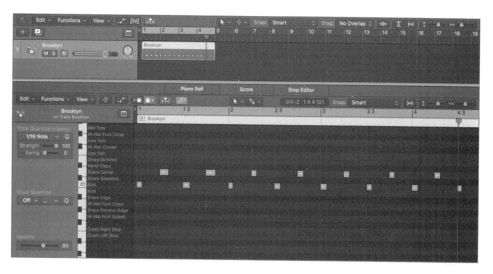

13 Play hi-hats on every eighth note using the F#1 (close hi-hat) and A#1 (open hi-hat) keys, playing the open hi-hat only as the last eighth note of some of the bars.

14 Stop recording, click the background of the Piano Roll to deselect the notes, and press Z.

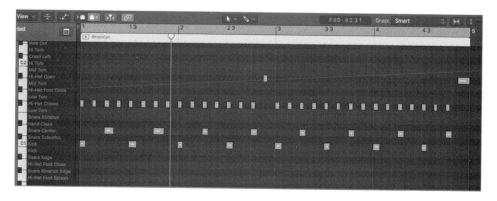

If the Piano Roll vertical zoom level allows, the drum names are displayed in front of the keyboard to the left of the grid. You can see your drum pattern. Now that the notes are not selected, you can see their colors, which vary depending on the note's velocity.

Joining MIDI recordings as you did in the two previous exercises provides a lot of flexibility and allows you to take your time, recording a single part of a performance at a time. These techniques will help in many situations. For example, consider first recording the notes of a cello melody, and then later recording the movements of the pitch bend wheel to add cello-like vibrato toward the end of sustained notes.

Recording MIDI Takes

When you want to nail a performance or experiment with several musical ideas, you can record multiple takes and later choose the best one. The techniques for recording MIDI takes are similar to the techniques you used to record audio takes in Lesson 2. You can record new takes over an existing region or take folder, or you can record multiple takes in Cycle mode.

Cycle mode should still be turned on from the previous exercise. Let's record takes in Cycle mode and experiment with using different melodies for a bass line.

1   Choose Record > Overlapping MIDI Recordings > Cycle On > Create Take Folder.

2   Choose Track > New Software Instrument Track (or press Command-Option-S).

3   Open the Library, and choose Bass > Stinger Bass.

4   Start playback and play a few notes on your MIDI keyboard.

   You can hear your bass, and you can practice until you find an idea for a simple bass line that will work with the drums you recorded on track 1.

► **About Live Mode**

Selecting a software instrument track automatically record-enables it, but the instrument is not always in Live mode (for example, when selecting a software instrument track during playback). An instrument in Live mode requires more CPU resources. When an instrument is not in Live mode, the first note you play will take about 100 ms (milliseconds) to trigger the instrument, which is then placed in Live mode.

You can put an instrument in Live mode by sending any MIDI event to it (playing a dummy note, moving the modulation wheel, and so on), by clicking the R button in the track header to make it solid red, or by starting playback.

Record-enabled instrument not in Live mode   Record-enabled instrument in Live mode

5   While playback continues, click the Record button (or press R). Logic continues repeating the cycle area, so you don't lose your groove.

6   When the playhead starts a new pass of the cycle, play a bass melody on the MIDI keyboard.

When you're done recording the four-bar bass melody, the playhead jumps back to the beginning of the cycle. You can continue recording new takes while staying in Cycle mode, or stop recording and start recording again to record new takes.

7   Record two more takes of the bass.

8   Start playback. You can hear the last take of the bass.

9   In the workspace, from the take folder pop-up menu, choose take 2.

You can hear take 2.

NOTE ▶ Note that there's no Quick Swipe Comping button next to the take folder pop-up menu. Unlike with audio take folders, you cannot comp sections of takes in a MIDI take folder.

10   Double-click the take folder to open it. Click the first take, at the bottom of the list, to play it.

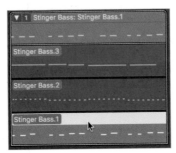

11 Choose your favorite take, and from the take folder pop-up menu, choose Flatten.

The take folder is flattened, and only the selected bass take remains in a MIDI region.

12 Stop playback.

> **TIP** ▶ If you want to keep a performance you played while Logic was in playback mode, click Stop and press Shift-R (Capture as Recording). A MIDI region containing your last performance is created on the track.

Lesson Review

1. How do you merge a new recording in an existing MIDI region?
2. How can you time-correct a MIDI region?
3. How do you choose default region parameters for new MIDI recording?
4. What type of Track Stack should you create to have MIDI regions on the main track trigger instruments on the subtracks?
5. In the Smart Controls pane, how do you map a screen control to a plug-in parameter?
6. In the Smart Controls pane, how do you assign a screen control to a knob on your MIDI controller?
7. How do you automatically arpeggiate chords?
8. How can you put a track into Live mode?

Answers

1. Choose Record > Overlapping MIDI Recordings > No Cycle > Merge; or if Cycle mode is on when you record, choose Record > Overlapping MIDI Recordings > Cycle > Merge.

2. In the Region inspector, set the Quantize parameter to the desired note length.

3. Deselect all regions in the workspace to access the MIDI Defaults settings in the Region inspector.

4. A summing stack.

5. In the Parameter Mapping area, click Learn. Click a screen control to select it, and click a plug-in parameter to map it to the selected screen control.

6. In the External Assignment area, click Learn. Click a screen control to select it, and turn a knob on your MIDI controller until the screen control moves along.

7. In the MIDI FX slot of the software instrument channel strip, insert the Arpeggiator MIDI effect plug-in.

8. Click its Record-enable button, or, for the selected track, send any MIDI event from your MIDI controller, or start playback.

Keyboard Shortcuts

Project

Command-Shift-N	Creates a new empty project
Command-Option-W	Closes the current project

Windows and Panes

Command-K	Opens or closes the Musical Typing window
P	Opens the Piano Roll
B	Opens the Smart Controls
V	Hides or shows all the plug-in windows

Tracks Area

Command-Option-S	Creates a new software instrument track
Command-Shift-D	Creates a Track Stack for the selected tracks

6

Lesson Files

Time

Goals

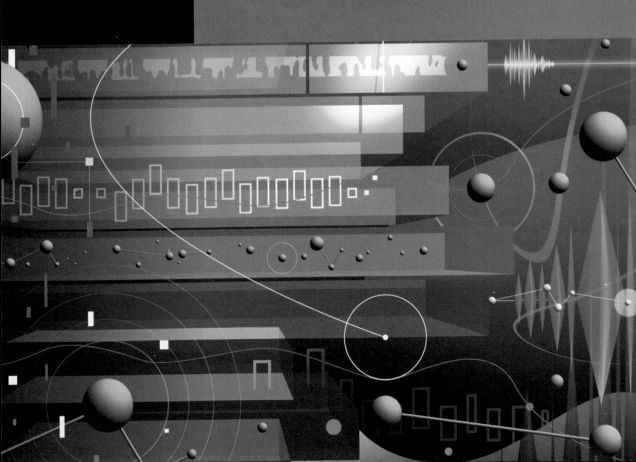

Creating and Editing MIDI

When you work with MIDI sequences, the flexibility of separating the performance data from a specific instrument gives you total control over the performance data, even after it is recorded. You can open the MIDI region in a MIDI editor to precisely fine-tune each note's position, pitch, velocity, and length. You can edit or add MIDI controller events to automate the instrument's volume, panning, pitch, and many other parameters. You can also write music from scratch, creating notes in MIDI editors using only your mouse, similar to the way you write music on staff paper.

Writing music in MIDI editors is also called *programming MIDI sequences.* Logic includes several MIDI editors for this purpose, and though they all display the same MIDI events, each does so in its own way. For example, the Score Editor shows you musical notes on a staff, and the Piano Roll Editor shows you notes as beams on a grid.

In this lesson, you will program and edit MIDI events using the Logic MIDI editors. You will write a bass line, import and edit a MIDI file triggering a synth patch, and program MIDI control automation to breathe life into your MIDI sequences.

Creating MIDI Notes in the Piano Roll Editor

The Piano Roll Editor is the most straightforward MIDI editor in Logic. Its name is inspired by the perforated paper roll used by mechanical player pianos, in which the position and length of those perforations determined the pitches and durations of notes.

In Logic, the Piano Roll Editor represents MIDI notes as beams on a grid, positioned below a bar ruler, much like the workspace displays regions on a grid below a bar ruler. In fact, most of the techniques for editing regions in the workspace also apply to notes in the Piano Roll Editor.

Creating and Resizing Notes

In the Piano Roll Editor, you create notes by clicking in the grid with the Pencil tool. As you write your musical part using the Pencil tool, you can also use the Pencil tool to resize, move, copy, or delete notes.

You will open a new project that has a basic rock drum track, create a new bass track, and use the Pencil tool to program a simple bass line in the Piano Roll.

1   Open Logic Pro X Files > Lessons > **06 Rock Drums**.

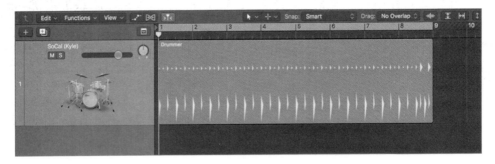

The project contains a single Drummer track cycling around for eight bars. Listen to the drums. They play a straightforward rock drum pattern with a simple fill at the end of the eight-bar pattern.

2   Choose Track > New Software Instrument Track (or press Command-Option-S).

3   In the control bar, click the Library button (or press Y).

4   In the Library, choose Bass > Stinger Bass.

5   In the control bar, click the Editors button. At the top of the Editors pane, ensure that Piano Roll is selected (or press P).

Let's make the Piano Roll taller.

6   Place the mouse pointer between the Piano Roll and the Tracks area and drag the resize pointer up.

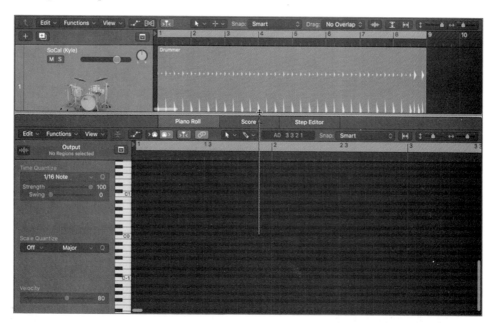

As you resize the Piano Roll, you may hide some of the tracks in the Tracks area. You can use Vertical Auto Zoom to maximize the track heights while keeping all tracks visible.

7   In the Tracks area menu bar, click the Vertical Auto Zoom button.

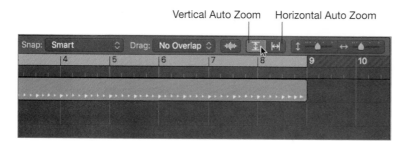

The tracks are automatically zoomed to fit vertically in the Tracks area.

8   Try resizing the Piano Roll to a comfortable size.

As you drag the resize pointer to adjust the height of the Piano Roll, the tracks automatically update their vertical zoom to fit the Tracks area.

9   In the Piano Roll, click the keys on the piano keyboard.

The keys trigger the bass instrument, and you can hear the bass notes.

As you position the mouse pointer over the grid, look at the info display at the top of the Piano Roll. Scroll down to find A1, two white keys below C2. On the grid, light gray lanes correspond to the white keys on the piano keyboard, whereas dark gray lanes correspond to the black keys.

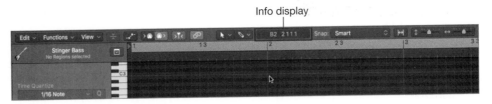

NOTE ▶ If you cannot see the info display, try making the main window wider or close side panes such as inspectors and browsers.

You will now use the Pencil tool, your current Command-click tool, to create notes.

10 Command-click the light gray lane at 1 1 1 1 next to the A1 key.

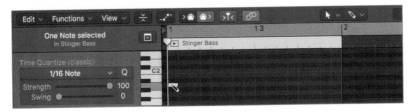

Clicking the grid with the Pencil tool inserts a note on the closest grid line to the left. For example, clicking at 1 1 1 181 inserts a note at 1 1 1 1.

NOTE ▶ The color of the note indicates its velocity. You will adjust note velocities later in this lesson.

By default, Logic creates a sixteenth note. In the Tracks area, a MIDI region named *Stinger Bass* is created on the bass track that contains that note. You will resize the note to an eighth note.

11 Position the pointer over the right edge of the note until it changes to a Resize tool.

12 Drag the Resize tool to the right to lengthen the note to an eighth note.

The help tag shows the note length as 0 0 2 0, which indicates that the length is 0 bars, 0 beats, 2 divisions, and 0 ticks. By default, the division is set to 1/16, so two divisions make an eighth note.

13 Command-click after the existing eighth note to create a new note at 1 1 3 1.

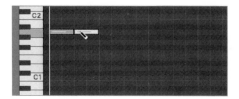

A new note is created with the same length as the previous eighth note.

NOTE ▶ When creating a note, the new note has the same length as the note you most recently created or selected.

You can check the pitch and velocity of a note by placing the pointer over the note. After a pause, a help tag appears with the information.

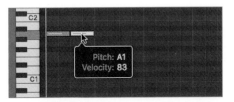

To check the position, length, and pitch of a note, you can click and hold the note.

This time you will create and resize a note in a single operation.

14 Using the Pencil tool, hold down the mouse button to create a C2 after the last note (at 1 2 1 1), and drag to the right to lengthen the note to a quarter note (0 1 0 0).

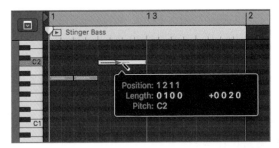

You now understand the basic tools for creating notes on the grid and how to adjust their lengths. In the next exercise, you will continue the musical motif using characteristics of the existing notes to create new notes.

Defining Note Length with Existing Notes

To finish this first bar, you will repeat the same rhythmic motif (two eighth notes followed by a quarter note) on new pitches. You'll select existing notes to create notes of the same length and velocity.

1   Click one of the two eighth notes at the beginning of the bar to select it.

From now on, clicking with the Pencil tool will create eighth notes.

2   Command-click to create a G1 at 1 3 1 1.

3   Command-click to create another G1 at 1 3 3 1.

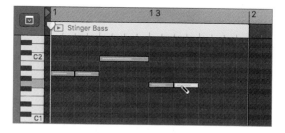

The next note you want to create is a quarter note, so first you will select a quarter note.

4   Click the quarter note on C2 to select it.

5   Create a B1 quarter note at 1 4 1 1.

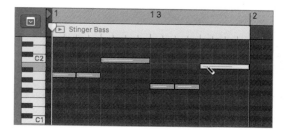

6   Play your bass line. The melody is nice, but the bass is played too legato.

7 Drag a rectangle around all the notes (or press Command-A) to select them.

8 Drag the right edge of one of the selected notes toward the left to shorten it slightly. After you start dragging, you can hold down Control to adjust the length with more precision.

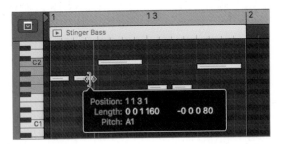

9 Listen to the bass line. You can hear the individual notes with more distinction now.

You now have a one-bar pattern. You could continue writing the bass line with the Pencil tool, but to go faster you'll repeat the pattern with small modifications to add variation.

10 Ensure that all the notes are selected, and choose Edit > Repeat (or press Command-R).

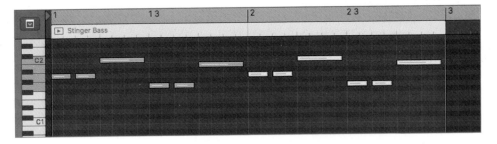

The pattern in bar 1 is repeated in bar 2, thereby extending the region by one bar. You will now replace the last quarter note of bar 2 with two eighth notes.

11 Click the background of the Piano Roll to deselect all the notes.

12 Select the last quarter note in bar 2 and press Delete.

13 Drag to select the two last eighth notes in bar 2.

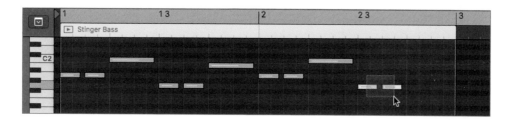

14 Choose Edit > Repeat (or press Command-R).

Two new eighth notes fill the last beat of bar 2. You will now repeat this two-bar pattern throughout the remaining six bars of the cycle area.

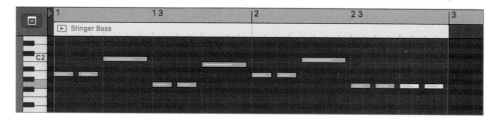

15 Press Command-A to select all the notes, and then press Command-R three times.

In the Tracks area, the *Stinger Bass* MIDI region extends to fill the eight bars of the cycle area.

16 Click the background of the Piano Roll, and press Z.

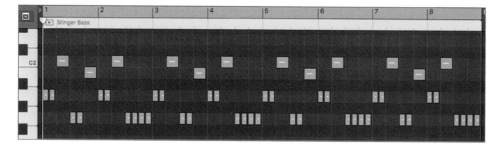

You can see your entire eight-bar bass line.

You used the Pencil tool to create notes, resize them, and define the length and velocity of new notes. Then you used the Repeat key command to quickly fill up an eight-bar region with your two-bar pattern. Right now, the bass line is rather repetitive, but you'll add small variations in the next exercise to make it more exciting.

Editing Note Pitch Using Key Commands

Creating notes with the Pencil tool is fine when you have a clear idea of the pitches you want. But sometimes you may want to experiment with different pitches while listening to the result.

In this exercise, you will use key commands to select some of the eighth notes at the end of every two-bar section and change their pitches.

1   Click the last eighth note of bar 2 to select it.

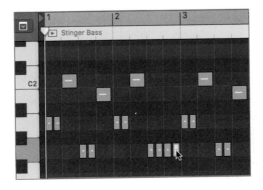

From now on, make sure the Piano Roll always has key focus. You will use the following key commands to select and transpose notes:

▶   Left/Right Arrow—Selects previous/next note

▶   Option-Up/Down Arrow—Transposes up/down one semitone

▶   Shift-Option-Up/Down Arrow—Transposes up/down one octave

NOTE ▶ If you happen to press Up Arrow by mistake, the Drummer track is selected and the Drummer Editor opens, replacing the Piano Roll. To resume working on the bass, press Down Arrow to reselect the bass track and to reopen the Piano Roll.

2   Press Option-Up Arrow.

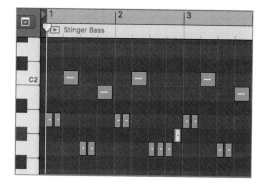

The note is transposed up one semitone (from a G1 to a G#1).

3   Press Left Arrow to select the previous note.

4   Press Option-Up Arrow.

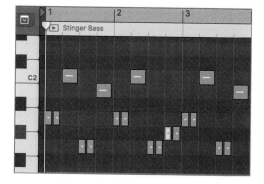

This note is also transposed up one semitone.

5   Press the Spacebar to listen to this new bass fill.

It renews interest at the end of the first two bars. The G# leads smoothly into the A at the beginning of the pattern in bar 3.

6   Keep the song playing for the next few steps; you will continue editing note pitches while listening to the song.

7   Press Right Arrow a few times.

Each time you press Right Arrow, the next note to the right is selected, and its sound is played. This can be distracting when you're trying to focus on the result of your edits.

8   At the top of the Piano Roll, click the MIDI Out button to turn off MIDI Out.

MIDI Out button

9   Press Right Arrow a few more times to select the next to last eighth note in bar 4.

With MIDI Out turned off, no sound is triggered as you select different notes, which makes hearing the song easier.

10 Press Option-Up Arrow four times to transpose the note four semitones higher (from a G1 to a B1).

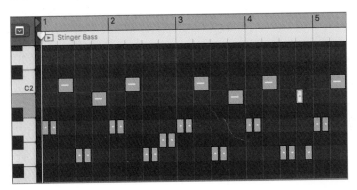

Continue using these key commands to edit the bass fills at the ends of bar 6 and bar 8, choosing pitches that sound good to you.

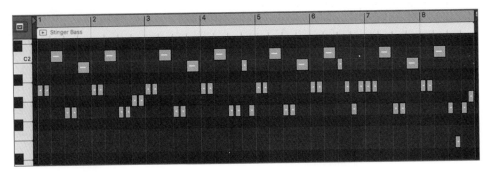

11 Stop playback.

You now have a bass line that repeats the same one-bar pattern for eight bars, with just enough variation in every other bar to keep things sounding fresh.

Editing Note Velocity

When you play a MIDI keyboard, you want to control how loud each note is played. To judge how hard you press the keys, MIDI keyboards measure the speed at which each key is depressed. That speed is called *velocity*. When you press a key, the MIDI keyboard sends a note on MIDI event that contains the key number and velocity value of that note.

Higher velocities usually result in louder notes. Depending on the patch or program you're using, higher velocities may also trigger different sounds or different samples, as they do in the sampler instrument you're using in the Stinger Bass track. Higher-velocity notes trigger samples of a bass string that was plucked harder, allowing you to program accents or dynamic variations that sound realistic.

In this exercise, you will use different techniques to change the velocities of notes in the bass line, thereby changing their volumes and timbres, and making your MIDI programming sound closer to a live performance.

1 At the top of the Piano Roll, click the MIDI Out button to enable MIDI Out.

2 Control-Option-drag to zoom in on the first three notes.

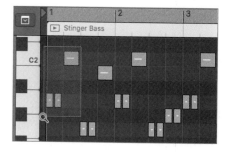

3 In the Left-click Tool menu at the top of the Piano Roll, choose the Velocity tool (or press T, and then press V).

TIP▶ You can also hold down Control-Command to temporarily turn the Pointer tool into the Velocity tool.

4   Using the Velocity tool, drag the first note up or down.

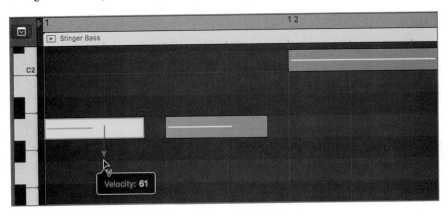

As you drag with the Velocity tool, the MIDI note is triggered repeatedly so that you can hear the sound of the note at different velocities. Notice how higher velocities trigger bass sounds that were plucked harder and have more attack.

The help tag displays the value of the velocity, from 1 to 127.

The velocity value is indicated by the color of the note, ranging from cold colors (low velocities) to warm colors (high velocities). Velocity is also represented by the length of the line in the middle of the note beam.

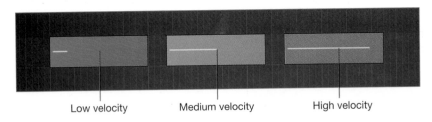

Low velocity   Medium velocity   High velocity

By default, all the notes you previously created have a velocity of 80.

You can add an accent to the first note, settling for, as an example, a velocity of 105. The first bass note is now a little louder.

Let's select all B1 and C2 notes and raise their velocities together.

5   Click the background of the Piano Roll, and press Z to zoom out.

6   On the piano keyboard, click the C2 key to select all C2 notes in the region.

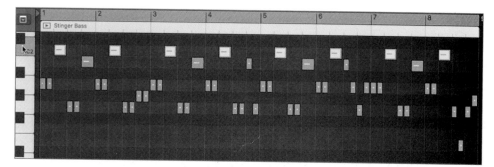

7   Shift-click the B1 key (just below C2) to add all B1 notes to your selection.

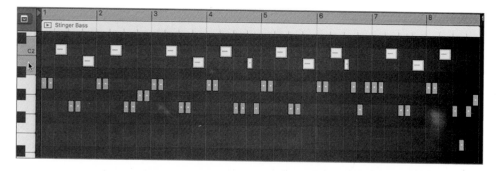

8   Using the Velocity tool, drag one of the selected notes to set the velocity of all the selected notes to 100.

> **NOTE ▶** When multiple selected notes have different velocities, dragging them with the Velocity tool offsets the velocities of all notes by the same amount, and the differences in velocity between the notes are retained.

9   Press T twice to change the Left-click tool to the Pointer tool.

10 Click the background to deselect the notes.

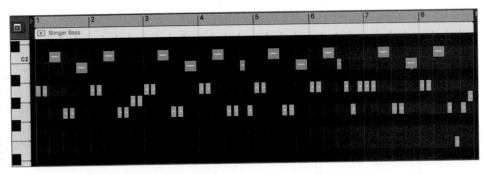

All C2 and B1 notes now have a warmer color because they all have a velocity of 100.

11 Listen to the song. The accents on the quarter notes help make the bass groove better.

Continue adjusting the velocities of individual notes in the bass fills you created in the previous exercise to make them stand out a little, especially at the end of bar 8, during the drum fill on the Drummer track.

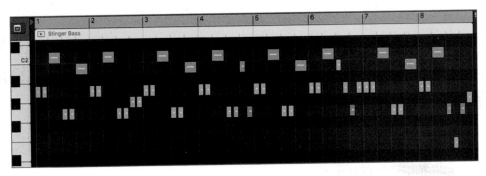

Creating and Drawing Note Patterns

Creating MIDI sequences one note at a time is not always the most efficient method. When a pattern contains repetitive elements, the Brush tool can help you create multiple notes in a single operation.

In this exercise, you will convert the Drummer region into a MIDI region so that you can add a clave pattern. You will paint MIDI notes using the Brush tool and drag the time handles to time-stretch some of the notes.

1   On track 1, Control-click the Drummer region, and from the shortcut menu, choose
    Convert > Convert to MIDI Region.

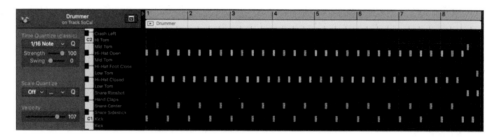

The Piano Roll displays the drum names in the local inspector. If you cannot see the
drum names, zoom in vertically in the Piano Roll.

2   Scroll up to see the Count-In/Clave (on D#4).

3   Control-Option-drag to zoom in on the first bar.

4   Press T to open the Tool menu, and choose the Brush tool.

5   Drag the Brush tool to paint sixteenth notes in beats 2 and 3.

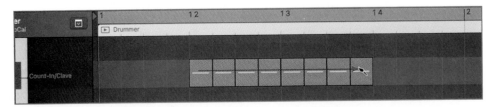

6   Listen to your clave pattern.

Even though all the MIDI notes are identical, Drum Kit Designer plays different samples every time to avoid the "machine gun" effect when a sampler plays a rapid succession of identical samples. Still, the pattern is rather simple so far. Let's slow down the last four notes.

7   From the Piano Roll menu bar, choose Functions > Time Handles, or press T.

8   Press T twice to change the Left-click tool to a Pointer tool.

9   Drag around the four notes in beat 3 to select them, with the time handles positioned on beats 3 and 4.

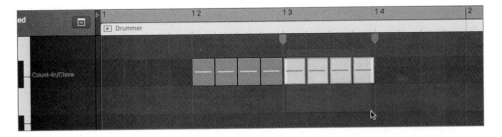

10   Drag the right time handle to the middle of beat 4.

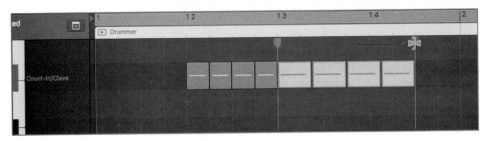

The selected notes are stretched.

11 Listen to the clave pattern.

The last four notes are played slower than the first four notes. You will now create a roll by deleting the first clave note and replacing it with four very fast notes.

12 Choose Functions > Time Handles, or press Control-T, to deselect the time handles.

13 Press T to open the Tool menu, and choose the Brush tool.

14 Position the Brush tool over the first clave note.

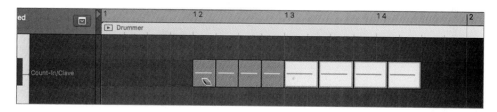

The Brush tool turns into an Eraser tool.

15 Click the note to erase it.

To change the length of the notes that the Brush tool creates, you will change the Time Quantize note value.

16 In the Piano Roll inspector, from the Time Quantize pop-up menu, choose 1/64 Note.

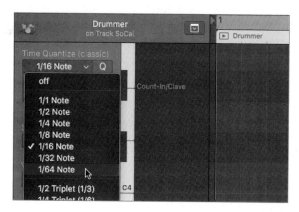

17 Drag the Brush tool to paint four sixty-fourth notes in the empty space at the beginning of the clave pattern.

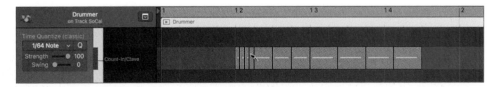

18 Listen to the clave pattern.

It starts with a fast roll, and then plays three sixteenth notes and slows down for the last four notes. You will now paint that same pattern in different locations in the MIDI region.

You have used the Brush tool to paint multiple identical notes, and you've defined the note lengths using the Time Quantize note value. The time handles allowed you to time-stretch some of the notes to customize your pattern.

Defining and Painting Custom Note Patterns

The Brush tool has some hidden power. You can select a note pattern you've created and define it as a brush pattern. You then drag the Brush tool to paint that custom pattern anywhere you'd like in the MIDI region.

1 In the Piano Roll inspector, click the Count-In/Clave name to select all the clave notes.

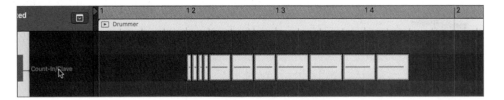

2   With the Brush tool, Control-click one of the selected notes, and from the shortcut menu, choose Define Brush Pattern.

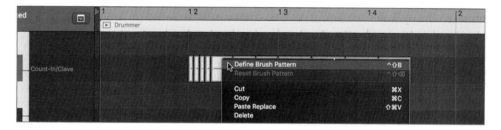

Before you paint more notes, it would be nice to be able to see all the notes in your MIDI region. However, zooming out vertically would make the notes very small, and the drum names would disappear. Instead, you will use Collapse mode, which displays lanes only when MIDI notes are present.

3   In the Piano Roll menu bar, click the Collapse Mode button.

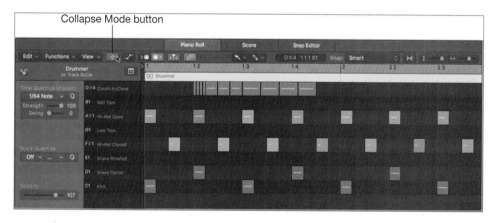

The Piano Roll displays only the eight lanes that contain MIDI notes, thereby allowing you to see the whole drum pattern.

4   Scroll to bar 3.

Dragging the Brush tool anywhere in the MIDI region will now paint that same pattern. If you hold down Shift while you paint a pattern, any vertical mouse movements will affect the velocity of the notes: dragging up will increase the velocity, and dragging down will decrease it.

5   On beat 2 of bar 3, click and hold the Brush tool, and then hold down Shift and drag the Brush tool toward the bottom right to paint the pattern while lowering the note velocities.

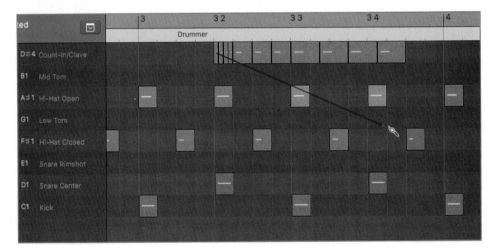

6   Listen to the clave pattern.

The second clave pattern has the same timing as the first pattern, but it is played softer.

7   Click the Collapse Mode button to turn it off.

8   Press T twice to change the Left-click tool to a Pointer tool.

You now know how to define your own custom brush pattern and paint it while varying the velocities of the notes. The Brush tool and the time handles come in handy whenever you're looking for an efficient way to create fast, original note patterns.

Importing a MIDI File

MIDI events recorded by software and hardware MIDI sequencers (including Logic) can be saved in standard MIDI file (SMF) format. Most sequencers can export and import standard MIDI files, which makes it easy to open them in multiple software sequencers or share them with others.

In the following exercise, you will import a MIDI file containing an eight-bar synth performance that you'll edit later in the Event List.

1   In the control bar, click the Browsers button (or press F), and at the top of the Browsers area, click All Files.

The All Files Browser displays all the files on your hard drive that can be used by Logic: audio files, MIDI files, movie files, and Logic and GarageBand projects.

2   At the top of the All Files Browser, click the Home button to list the contents of your home folder.

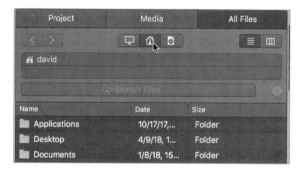

3   Navigate to Desktop > Logic Pro X Files > Media > Additional Media, drag
     Lead Synth.mid to bar 1 at the bottom of the workspace, and in the dialog asking
     if you want to import tempo information, click No.

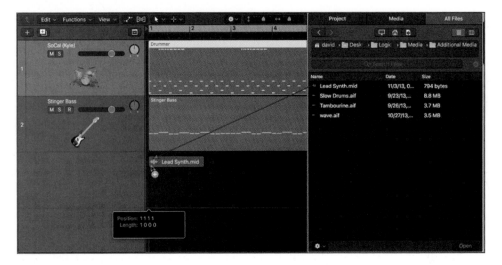

A new software instrument track is created, and a Steinway Grand Piano patch is
loaded by default. An eight-bar region named *Lead Synth* is created on the track. The
gray vertical bars in the region represent MIDI control events.

4   Listen to the song.

     You can hear a piano, which is the default instrument when you import a MIDI file.
     However, this sequence should be played by a synth.

5   Select the Steinway Grand Piano track, and in the Library, choose Synthesizer >
     Lead > Citrus Fuzz. Listen to the song.

     The synth plays a lot of fast notes, and then plays a very simple melody. You will
     breathe new life into the synth performance later in this lesson by inserting your own
     controller events.

     Notice that the synth is panned to the left and a little too low in volume.

6   In the Citrus Fuzz track header, drag the Volume slider up, and drag the Pan knob to the center position.

7   Start playback.

As the playhead jumps to bar 1 (the beginning of the cycle area) and playback starts, the Volume slider and the Pan knob revert to their original positions. MIDI files can contain controller volume and pan events, and when Logic plays those events, it uses them to set the volume and pan of the track. You'll later delete them in the Event List.

8   Stop playback, and press Return to go to the beginning of the song.

> **TIP** ▶ To export a MIDI region(s) as a standard MIDI file, select the region(s) in the workspace and choose File > Export > Selection as MIDI File.

Editing MIDI Data in the Event List

The Event List shows MIDI events as text and numbers. Unlike other MIDI editors—such as the Piano Roll Editor or the Score Editor—that can be more convenient for creative tasks, the Event List displays all the MIDI events in a region, along with the exact numerical values of their attributes (such as MIDI channel, key number, velocity, and so on). Although you probably won't use the Event List to compose, it can be a very powerful troubleshooting tool.

You will now open a MIDI file (that you imported in the previous exercise) in the Event List to locate and delete those MIDI events that are displayed as gray vertical bars on the MIDI region in the Tracks area.

1   In the control bar, click the Lists button to open the Event List.

Lists button

Event type buttons

The Event List displays all the MIDI events inside the selected *Lead Synth* region. You can see Control, Note, and C-Press (channel pressure, or aftertouch) events. A thin white horizontal playhead scrolls the events during playback. At the top of the Event List, the first two MIDI events are a volume event and a pan event. They are responsible for setting a specific volume and pan to the channel strip when playing that region. Let's delete all MIDI events that are not notes.

You can use the event type buttons to filter the events displayed.

2   Click the Notes event type button to disable it.

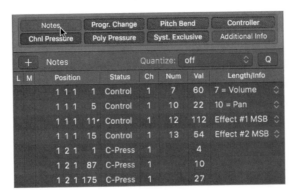

Note events are hidden. You will now delete all the Control and C-Press events.

3   In the Event List, choose Edit > Select > All (or press Command-A).

4   Choose Edit > Delete (or press Delete) to delete all the Control and C-Press events.

5   Click the Notes event type button to enable it.

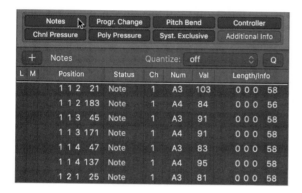

Notice that only Note events remain in the *Lead Synth* region.

6   Raise the volume and center the pan of the Citrus Fuzz track, and listen to the song.

This time the Volume slider and Pan knob in the track header stay put, and you can hear your synth loud and centered.

You won't turn to the Event List for everyday music creation, but it can be a powerful tool to display all the MIDI events inside a region in a single list—when locating and deleting unnecessary MIDI events, for example.

Quantizing Pitches and Timings of MIDI Notes

In this exercise you will quantize note pitches to certain keys and scales, forcing them to snap to the nearest note in that key. You will also quantize their timings to a grid, and adjust the strength of the quantizations to retain some of the human feel from the original performance.

1   In the workspace, click the *Lead Synth* region to display it in the Piano Roll Editor.

2 Press Z to see all the notes in the region.

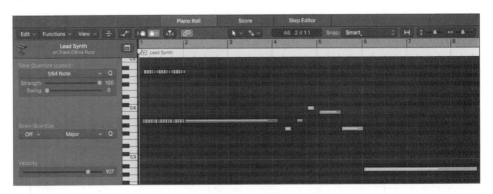

3 Select all five notes in bars 4 and 5.

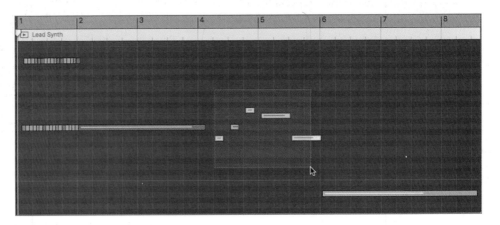

Let's try to play the selected notes in another key.

4 In the Piano Roll inspector, from the left Scale Quantize pop-up menu, choose A. Listen to the song.

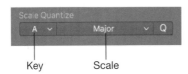

The notes jump to pitches in the key of A Major. You can use the Scale Quantize feature to experiment with playing a melody or chord progression in different keys. In this case, though, the original notes worked best.

5   From the Scale Quantize pop-up menu, choose Off to return the notes to their original pitches. Listen to the song again.

This time pay attention to the timing of the selected notes. It sounds as if the notes are really behind the beat.

6   Press Z to zoom in on the selected notes.

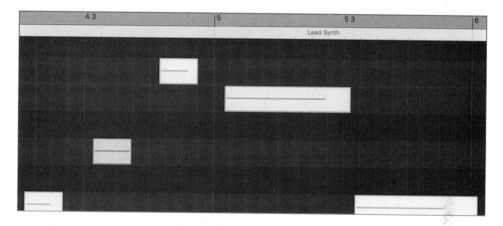

On the grid, you can see that the notes start late.

7   In the Piano Roll inspector, from the Time Quantize pop-up menu, choose 1/4 Note.

The selected notes snap to the nearest beat.

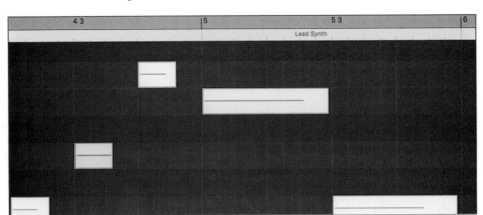

Listen to the song. The notes you've quantized are perfectly in time. But rather than snapping the notes to a rigid grid, you want to retain some of the original feel using the Time Quantize Strength slider.

As the song plays, the Piano Roll constantly updates its display to show the position of the playhead. After you've stopped playback, the notes you wanted to see are still selected, so you can press Z to bring them back into view.

8   Press Z. The selected notes fill the Piano Roll.

9   In the Piano Roll inspector, drag the Strength slider down to 50.

The notes are now positioned halfway between their original positions and the nearest quarter note on the grid.

10 In the Piano Roll, click the background to deselect all notes, and press Z to display all the notes. Listen to the song.

The synth's timing sounds better, but it still retains a bit of its original laid-back feel.

Creating a Crescendo Using Note Velocity

In the following exercise, you will employ a new technique to edit the velocity of the very fast notes at the beginning of the synth region, and make them play a crescendo (scaling note velocities from lower to higher values).

1   At the top of the Piano Roll, click the Show/Hide Automation button.

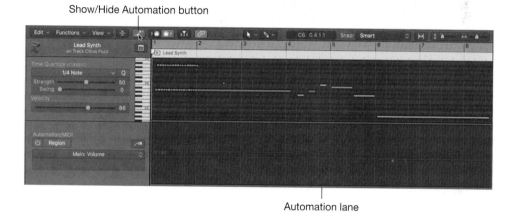

Show/Hide Automation button

Automation lane

The Automation lane opens at the bottom of the Piano Roll.

TIP ▶ If you need more display space to work in, choose Window > Open Piano Roll (or press Command-4) to open a full-screen Piano Roll window.

By default, the Automation lane displays Volume automation. However, let's switch it to view note velocity data instead.

2   Click the Automation Parameter pop-up menu, and in the MIDI area, choose Note Velocity.

Automation Parameter pop-up menu

The Automation lane displays the velocity of each MIDI note as a point, along with a line representing the length of the note. The height of each point represents the velocity of the note above it on the grid. You adjust the velocity of a note by vertically dragging the point (not the line).

3   Drag up the point of the first note in bar 4 to raise its velocity.

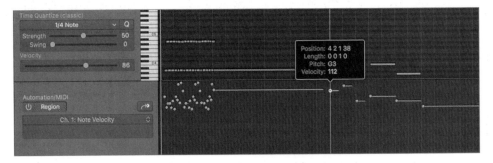

As you drag the point, a help tag shows you the position, length, pitch, and velocity of the note. When you release the mouse button, the color of the note beam in the Piano Roll updates to reflect the new velocity.

4   Listen to the fast notes at the beginning.

They all sound fairly loud. You will now draw a line in the Automation lane to create a crescendo in bar 1.

5   In the Automation lane, drag with the pointer to draw a line up from the lower left to the beginning of the long, sustained note at bar 2.

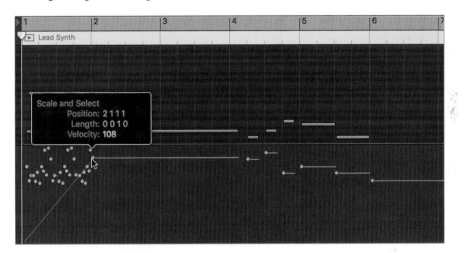

The note velocities are aligned to the green line you drew. In the Piano Roll, the notes with changed velocities are selected.

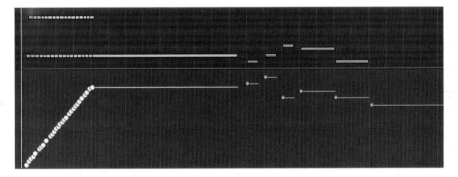

6   Listen to the synth. You can hear the notes crescendo; however, the first few notes are very soft, and you can barely hear them.

Let's raise the velocity of all the notes while keeping the crescendo you just drew.

7   In the Piano Roll inspector, drag the Velocity slider as far up as it can go, and listen to the synth.

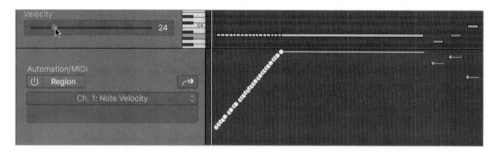

The velocities of all the selected notes are raised by the same amount, and the crescendo is now louder. In fact, the crescendo could use a gentler slope so that the sustained note in bar 2 doesn't have such a high velocity.

8   With the notes still selected, in the Automation lane, drag down the point of the sustained note at bar 2.

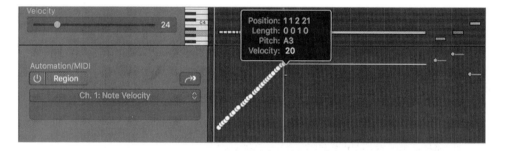

This time the note velocities are adjusted proportionately. For example, if you dragged one selected note velocity to half of its value, then the velocities of all the other selected notes are also halved. This gives your crescendo a gentler slope.

9   Listen to the synth. It is now easier to hear the first few notes, but the last note is no longer too loud.

TIP   You will learn how to use automation in the Tracks area in Lesson 10.

Creating and Editing MIDI Continuous Controllers

When playing a MIDI keyboard, you can add expression to your performance by using the physical knobs, sliders, wheels (such as the pitch bend and modulation wheels), and volume pedal. Manipulating those controllers sends a stream of control events that represent the movement of the controller knob and trigger an action on the instrument.

When programming MIDI, you can draw a stream of control events to alter an instrument's volume, pitch, and other parameters. In the following exercises, you will use the Logic MIDI editors to automate pitch bend and modulation in the synth MIDI region.

Automating Pitch Bend Data

Adding pitch glides at the beginnings or ends of notes can make a MIDI sequence sound musical. Let's enliven your synth performance by bending the pitch in various places and adding a vibrato at the end of a sustained note.

1   Click the Automation Parameter pop-up menu, and in the MIDI area, choose
    Pitch Bend.

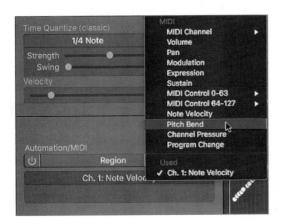

The Automation lane shows an empty canvas (note velocity data is still visible by transparency), ready for you to draw pitch bend automation. First, you will draw a pitch drop from the beginning to the end of the fast notes in bar 1.

2   At the upper left of the Automation lane, click to create a point.

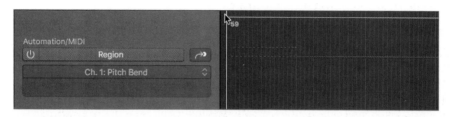

Predicting the exact position and value of a point you create can be a bit tricky. To adjust a point, drag it using the Pointer tool.

TIP ▸ After creating the first point, click the automation line, or double-click away from the automation line, to create a new point. You can also create points by clicking or dragging with the Pencil tool.

3   In the lower part of the Automation lane, double-click at bar 2 to get the lowest value possible. Listen to the first bar of the synth.

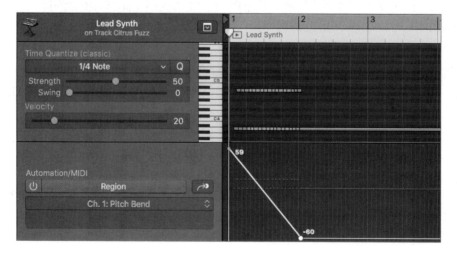

You can hear the fast notes drop in pitch throughout bar 1. However, the rest of the notes play at the wrong pitch. To play the remaining notes at their correct pitches, you must return the pitch to the position of the 0 value (the center position on a MIDI keyboard's Pitch Bend wheel).

4   A little before bar 3, click to create a point on the horizontal green line that has the same value as the previous point you created.

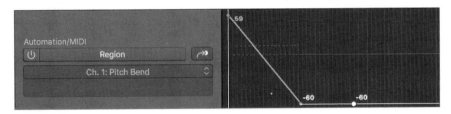

TIP▶ To delete a point, double-click it with the Pointer tool. To delete multiple points, drag around them to select them, and then press Delete on your keyboard.

5   A little after bar 3, create a point, and drag it to a value of 0. Listen to the synth.

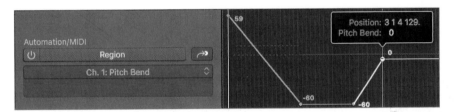

The pitches of the fast notes in bar 1 drop over a range of four semitones; then the sustained note is bent at bar 3, going back up two semitones. You will make the pitch variations more pronounced by increasing the pitch bend range.

The MIDI pitch bend events do not include any pitch bend range information, so it's up to the instrument receiving the events to determine which pitch bend range to use. As with the instrument used here, most instruments default to a range of two semitones above or below the original pitch. And most instruments allow you to adjust the pitch bend range. You will now open the ES2 instrument plug-in on the Citrus Fuzz channel strip in the inspector to adjust its pitch bend range.

6   On the Citrus Fuzz channel strip, click the middle of the Instrument slot.

The ES2 plug-in opens.

Pitch bend range

7   In the ES2, drag the upward Bend range field to 12 semitones (one octave).

Upward Bend range

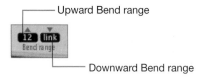

Downward Bend range

The downward Bend range field is set to *link,* which means that the downward Bend range value is set the same as the upward Bend range value. You can now bend notes up to one octave above or one octave below the original pitch.

8   Listen to the synth. The fast notes at the beginning drop two octaves; then the sustained note comes back up one octave to the original pitch.

However, unless you got very lucky, the beginning of the sustained note sounds out of tune. You most likely need to adjust the pitch bend value in that section to make sure that it is all the way down (so that part of the note is exactly one octave lower than the original pitch of the note).

9   Close the ES2 plug-in window (or press Command-W).

10 In the Automation lane, drag down the horizontal line between the two points in bar 2 all the way to a value of –64. Listen to the synth again.

This time the beginning of that sustained note sounds in key, exactly one octave below the original pitch.

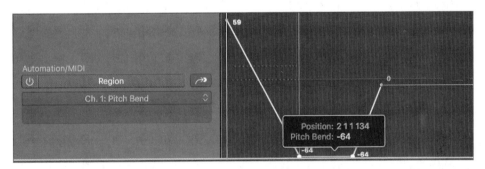

Holding down Control-Shift turns the pointer into an Automation Curve tool that you can use to curve the lines joining two points of different values. (You can't curve a horizontal line.)

11 Control-Shift-drag the line between the –64 and 0 values (around bar 3).

Drag up or down to create a convex or concave curve, respectively. Drag left or right to create a horizontal or vertical S curve, respectively.

TIP ▶ To create more complex shapes, drag the Pencil tool to draw the desired automation.

12 Control-Shift-drag that same line to the right to create an S curve.

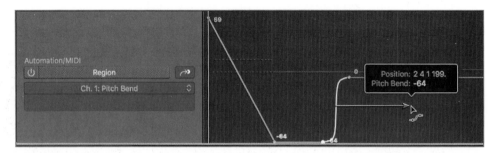

The pitch glide in the middle of the sustained note is now a little faster.

TIP ▶ In the Automation lane, Control-Shift-click a curved line to revert to a straight line.

Copying MIDI Control Data

Let's continue automating the pitch bend data in the *Lead Synth* region. You will raise the next three notes in bar 4 from lower pitches to their correct pitches at the beginning of each note. You will create the desired pitch bend automation for one note, and copy it to the two other notes.

1 In the Piano Roll, zoom in on the three quarter notes in bar 4.

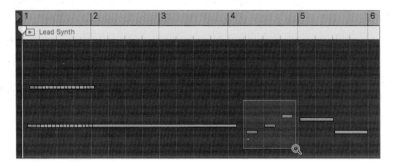

2   Click the green line to create a point to the left of the first note, and make sure it has a value of 0.

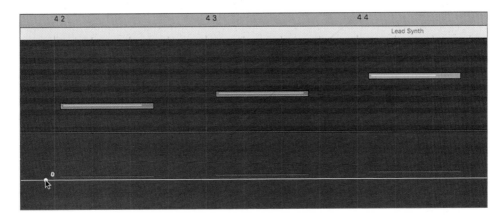

3   Create a point about halfway down, and drag it horizontally between the previous point and the beginning of the note.

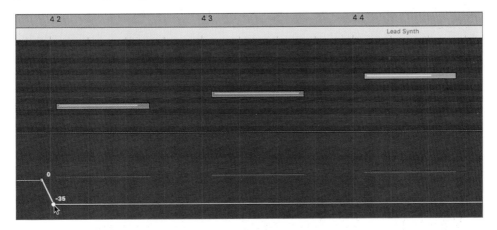

4 Create a point a little before the middle of the note with a value of 0. Listen to your synth.

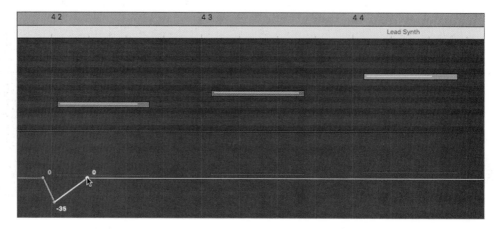

The note now starts on a low pitch and raises to the correct pitch (similar to the way Frank Sinatra often glided up into the correct pitch).

You will now copy the same pitch bend automation to the two following notes.

5 At the bottom of the Piano Roll, drag the horizontal scroll bar to scroll back to the three notes in bar 4.

6 Drag a selection rectangle around the three points at the beginning of the first note.

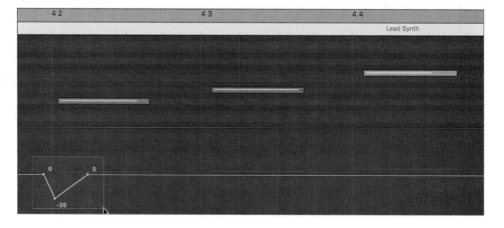

7   Option-drag the selected pitch bend data to the beginning of the second note.

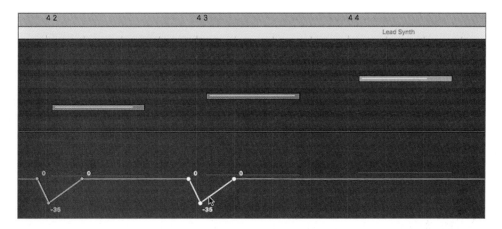

8   Option-drag the selected pitch bend data below the second note to the beginning of the third note. Listen to your synth.

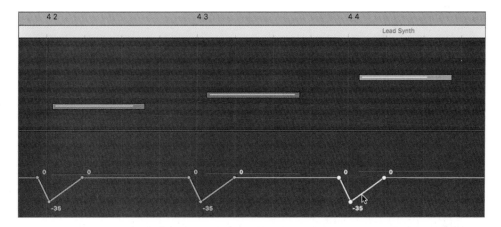

All three notes are raised to their correct pitches at the beginning of each note, which makes them more expressive.

9   Using the techniques you've learned in this exercise, drop down the pitch of the last sustained note in the region an entire octave before the end of the note (around bar 8).

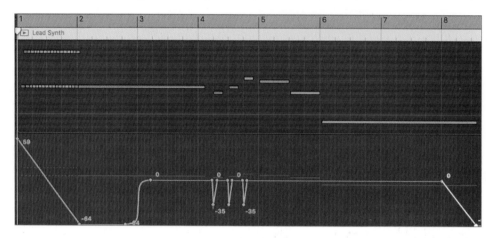

Automating Modulation Data

When listening to singers or string players, you may notice that they often use vibrato, and tend to use it more toward the end of sustained notes. On synthesizers, the modulation wheel (often located to the left of the keys) frequently controls the depth of the vibrato. You will now add some modulation automation to the synth to add vibrato to the end of the first sustained note.

1   From the Automation Parameter pop-up menu, in the MIDI area, choose Modulation.

2   At the beginning of the region, click the very bottom of the Automation lane to create a point with a value of 0.

3   Click the line at bar 3 to create a point with a value of 0.

4   In the middle of bar 3, at the very top of the Automation lane, double-click to create a point with a value of 126. Listen to your synth.

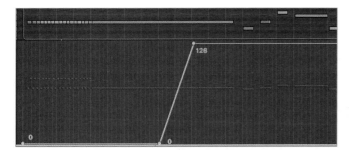

You can hear the vibrato effect come in after the sustained note's pitch goes up an octave at bar 3. However, the vibrato currently stays at its maximum value for the remainder of the region.

5   Create a point with a value of 126 right after the end of the sustained note.

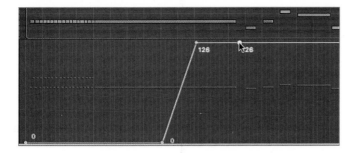

6   Create a point with a value of 0 after the point you just created, but before the beginning of the next note. Listen to your synth.

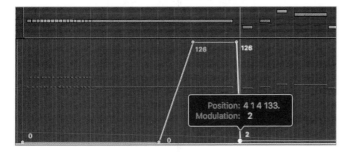

> **TIP** ▶ When dragging a point, a vertical guide line allows you to position the point in relation to the positions of notes in the Piano Roll.

Now the vibrato applies only to the first sustained note, and the next notes don't have any. This synth is now much more expressive than it was when you originally imported its MIDI file into the project. You will now add some audio effects to give even more life to the sound.

7   In the control bar, click the Smart Controls button (or press B).

8   Drag the Delay knob to about three quarters of its range, and drag the Scream knob halfway up.

9   Listen to the song and adjust other Smart Controls knobs as you listen to their effect on the synth sound.

10   Now that you're done editing the synth, you can turn its volume down (try about –10 dB). It may seem like the mix is weaker, so turn up your monitoring level on your audio interface (or by clicking the speaker icon in the Mac main menu bar) to compensate.

Bringing down the synth should enable you to more clearly hear the drums and bass.

In this lesson, you used two MIDI editors—the Piano Roll Editor and the Event List—to create and edit note and control data. But they can do so much more! The MIDI editors in Logic are powerful tools that include numerous options and features.

When trying to perform a specific task, don't hesitate to look through an editor's local menu, or to Control-click an event or an area of the editor to access the shortcut menus. Chances are, you will find the feature you are looking for and discover even more useful features you wouldn't have imagined.

Lesson Review

1. How do you create notes in the Piano Roll Editor?

2. How do you adjust note lengths in the Piano Roll Editor?

3. How do you adjust the velocity of notes in the Piano Roll Editor?

4. In the Piano Roll Editor, how do you view only those lanes occupied by MIDI notes?

5. How do you quickly paint multiple notes of the same length?

6. How do you create a crescendo using note velocities?

7. How do you create MIDI control data?

8. How do you curve lines in the Automation lane?

9. How do you copy a section of automation in the Automation lane?

10. How can you check the pitch and velocity of a note in the Piano Roll?

11. How can you check the position, length, and pitch of a note in the Piano Roll?

Answers

1. Click with the Pencil tool.

2. Drag the right edge of the note beam to resize the note.

3. Drag notes vertically with the Velocity tool.

4. Click the Collapse Mode button.

5. Drag the Brush tool.

6. In the Automation Parameter pop-up menu, ensure that Note Velocity is chosen, and draw a line in the Automation lane.

7. Choose a controller in the Automation Parameter pop-up menu, and click to create the first point. After at least one point is created, click the automation line, or double-click away from the automation line, to create a new point.

8. Hold down Control-Shift and drag a line between two points of different values.

9. Drag a rectangle around points to select them, and Option-drag the selection.

10. Place the pointer over the note. After a pause, a help tag appears with the information.

11. Click and hold the note.

Keyboard Shortcuts

Editing

Command-A	Selects all

Piano Roll

Left Arrow	Selects the note to the left of the selected note
Right Arrow	Selects the note to the right of the selected note
Option-Up Arrow	Transposes the selected note up one semitone
Option-Down Arrow	Transposes the selected note down one semitone
Shift-Option-Up Arrow	Transposes the selected note up one octave
Shift-Option-Down Arrow	Transposes the selected note down one octave

Windows and Panes

E	Opens the Editors area
F	Opens the Browsers area
Command-4	Opens a Piano Roll window

Building a Song

7

Lesson Files

Time   This lesson takes approximately 90 minutes to complete.

Goals   Match a project tempo to an audio file's tempo

Create Apple Loops

Add tempo changes and tempo curves

Apply tape or turntable speed-up and slow-down effects

Make one track follow the groove of another track

Use Varispeed effects

Edit the timing of an audio region

Edit note pitches in an audio region

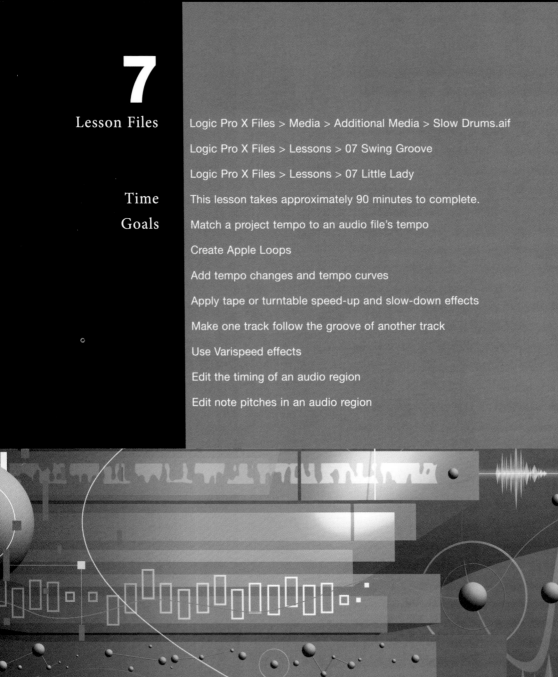

Editing Pitch and Time

The use of loops and samples has become omnipresent in modern music. New technologies encourage experimentation, and it is more and more common to find, say, a sample of a Middle Eastern instrument in a modern rock song, a sample of classical music in a pop song, or a sample of a pop song in a hip-hop track.

Mixing prerecorded material into a project can lead to exciting results, but the material must be carefully selected to ensure that it seamlessly blends into the project. The first challenge is to match the prerecorded musical material's tempo with the project's tempo.

Even when you record your own performances, precisely correcting the pitch and timing of an individual note can help you realize the perfection expected by a demanding audience. You can use note correction to fix imprecisions (or mistakes) in the recording, or you can use it creatively. Furthermore, special effects such as Varispeed and tape speed-up or slow-down can provide new inspiration.

In this lesson, you will match the tempo and groove of audio files to make sure they combine into a musical whole. You'll manipulate the project tempo to add tempo changes and tempo curves, apply Varispeed and Speed Fade effects, and use Flex editing to precisely adjust the position and length of individual notes and correct the pitch of a vocal recording.

Setting a Project Tempo by Detecting the Tempo of a Recording

While listening to various recordings, you've found a recording of drums you like because of the way it grooves at its original tempo. To build a project around it, you need to adjust the project's tempo to match the recording. When the two tempos match, you can use the grid to edit and quantize regions, or add Apple Loops and keep everything synchronized.

In this exercise, you will import a drums recording into a new project, let Logic detect the tempo of the drums, and set it as the project tempo.

1   Choose File > New, or press Shift-Command-N, and create one audio track.

    You will now set up Smart Tempo so that Logic detects the tempo of the audio file that you import, and sets the project tempo accordingly.

2   Click the Project Tempo pop-up menu, and choose ADAPT–Adapt Project Tempo.

    The global tempo track opens so you can easily spot any tempo changes that Logic may create. The tempo curve is orange, and in the LCD display, the project tempo and time signature are also orange, indicating that those parameters are ready to adapt to the audio file you're about to import.

3   In the control bar, click the Browsers button, or press F.

4   With the All Files tab selected, navigate to Desktop > Logic Pro X Files > Media > Additional Media, and drag **Slow Drums.aif** to bar 1 on the audio track.

An alert asks if you want to open the File Tempo Editor, which will allow you to refine Logic's tempo detection. Let's open it.

NOTE ▶ If Logic has previously analyzed this audio file (for example if you've already done this lesson), this alert won't appear. To remove the analysis information embedded in the audio file, choose Edit > Tempo > Remove Original Recording Tempo from Audio File.

5   Click Show.

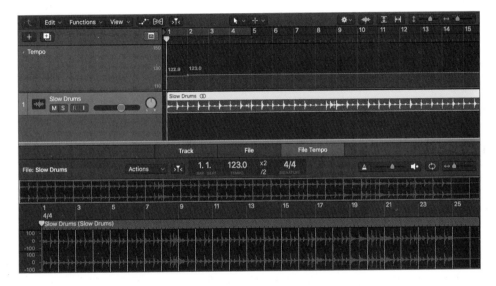

Two tempo changes are created: a tempo change of 122.9996 bpm at bar 1, and another of 123.0011 bpm at bar 2. In the global tempo track, Logic shows rounded tempo values of 122.9 and 123.0.

NOTE ▶ To see the exact tempo value of a section, click the arrow button at the lower-right of the LCD display, and choose Custom. Then locate the playhead in the desired section.

6   In the control bar, click the Metronome button, or press K.

7   Listen to the song.

The drums are in sync with the metronome; however, they actually play at half the speed. You can correct this in the File Tempo editor.

8   In File Tempo editor, click the /2 button.

The global tempo track now displays both tempo changes' rounded values as 61.5.

9   Listen to the song. Now the drums are perfectly in sync with the metronome.

10   In the Control bar, click the Editors button, or press E, to close the File Tempo editors.

11   In the LCD display, click the Project Tempo mode, and choose KEEP–Keep Project Tempo.

12   Click the Metronome button, or press K, to turn the metronome off.

Now that you've set the project tempo to match the drums tempo, you can add Apple Loops and they will automatically match the tempo of your drums. You can also use the grid in the workspace to cut an exact numbers of bars in a region, which you'll need later in this lesson to cut a drum loop.

Using and Creating Apple Loops

Apple Loops are AIFF or CAF format audio files containing additional information that allows them to automatically match the tempo and key when they're imported into a Logic project. They also contain descriptive information (such as instrument, mood, genre, and scale) that helps you search the vast library of loops using the Loop Browser.

Using the Loop Browser

You were introduced to the Loop Browser in Lesson 1 when you previewed and chose loops to create a project. You will now use it to add an Apple Loop to your drums track.

1   In the control bar, click the Apple Loops button (or press O).

2   At the top of the Loop Browser, click the Instrument button.

Let's try to find a bass loop.

3   Click the Elec Bass keyword button.

4   At the top of the Loop Browser, click the Genre button.

Your instrument category selection is retained, and you can further refine the search by genre.

5   Click the Chillwave keyword button.

The result lists display only electric bass loops in the Chillwave genre. Feel free to preview a few of the loops before moving on.

6   Drag Brooklyn Nights Bass to the workspace, below the drums track at bar 1.

7   Place the mouse pointer over the upper-right edge of the *Brooklyn Nights Bass* region. When the pointer turns into the Loop tool, drag to loop the region until bar 13.

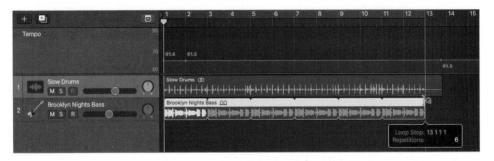

8   Listen to the song. The bass loop plays in sync with the project tempo, which means it's in sync with the drums. The bass loop is playing in the key of the project, C. In the next exercise you'll change the project key.

9   At the upper left in the Loop browser, click the X button to reset all keyword buttons.

Setting a Project's Key Signature

Loops generally sound more natural when they're played in their original keys. Their sound is closer to their producer's original intention, and with no transposition to process, the timbre of the loop is closest to the original recording and you hear fewer artifacts (distortion resulting from the time-stretching or pitch-shifting process).

Let's change the key of the project to E minor, which will make the bass sound a little more defined and less boomy.

1   In the control bar, click the Lists button.

2   At the top of the Lists area, click the Signature tab.

The Signature list shows the Time and Key signatures. The default key signature is C major.

3   In the Value column, click the key signature (C major), and from the pop-up menu, choose E minor.

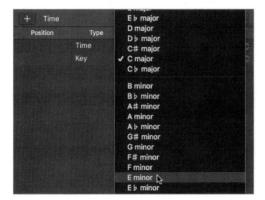

The Key signature is now E minor.

4   Click the Lists button to close the Signature list.

5   Listen to your song. The Brooklyn Nights Bass plays in the new project key, E.

Creating Apple Loops

When you want to catalog a section of an audio recording so you can reuse it in future projects, you can save it as an Apple Loop. The Apple Loop will be indexed in the Loop Browser so that you can easily find it later, and it will automatically match the tempo (and, when appropriate, the key) of the project into which you import the loop.

In the next exercise, you will first divide four bars of drums and then save them as a new Apple Loop.

1   Command-drag to select the four bars in the *Slow Drums* region, from 5 1 1 1 to 9 1 1 1.

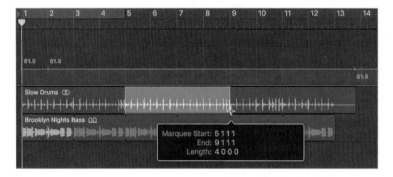

2   In the control bar, click the Apple Loops button (or press O) to open the Loop Browser.

3   Using the Pointer tool, drag the selected section of the drums to the Loop Browser.

As soon as you click the marquee selection, it is divided as a new region. When you release the mouse button over the Loop Browser, the "Add Region to Apple Loops Library" dialog opens.

4   In the dialog, enter or choose the following:

▶ Name: *Slow Drums*

▶ Type: Loop

▶ Scale: Good for Both

▶ Genre: Rock/Blues

▶ Descriptors: All Drums > Kits

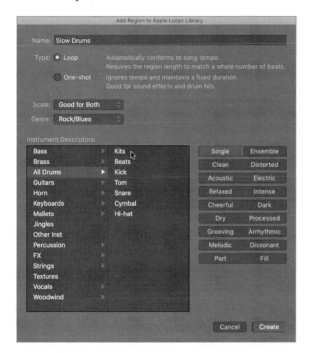

5   Click the Single, Clean, Acoustic, Dry, Grooving, and Part descriptor buttons. Descriptors determine which keyword buttons you'll later select in the Loop Browser to find that loop.

NOTE ▶ When dragging a region to the Loop Browser, you can create loops only when the number of beats in the region is an integer. This function uses the project tempo to tag the transient positions and works best for audio files that match the project tempo. If the selected region's number of beats is not an integer, the Type parameter will be set to One-shot and dimmed, and the resulting Apple Loop will not automatically match a project's tempo and key.

6   Click Create.

Logic bounces the section as a new Apple Loop and indexes it in the Loop Browser. Let's try to find it.

7   In the Loop Browser, in the search field, type *Slow Drums*.

The new Slow Drums Apple Loop that you just created is displayed in the lists result. Let's use that loop to replace the original drum recording you imported on track 1.

8   Click the Slow Drums track header.

All the regions on your selected track are also selected. Let's clear the track to make room for the new Apple Loop.

9   Press Delete.

10 Drag the new Slow Drums Apple Loop to the Slow Drums track.

11 Loop the drum loop to bar 13 so it ends at the same position as the bass loop.

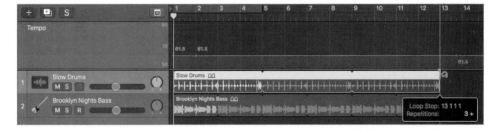

12 Play the project.

The drum and bass Apple Loops on both tracks play in sync. The drums stop abruptly at bar 13, so let's add a cymbal hit to punctuate the ending.

13 In the Loop browser, in the search field, enter *cymbal*.

14 Drag Long Crash Cymbal 02 below the bass track at bar 13.

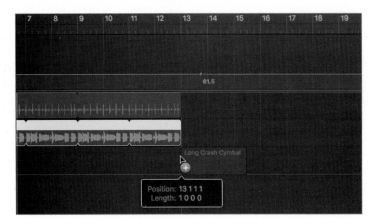

15 Close the Loop Browser.

> **NOTE ▶** You can also drag a MIDI region on a software instrument track to the Loop Browser to create a green Apple Loop. As with the blue Apple Loops you've already used, you can apply green Apple Loops as audio regions on audio tracks, or as MIDI regions on software instrument tracks, giving you the additional flexibility of being able to edit the sound of the instrument and the MIDI events.

Matching an Audio File to the Project Key and Tempo

Many current music genres find inspiration in older music, and it's common for producers to use samples of older recordings, whether for a vocal part or an orchestra hit. Recycling existing material to use in a new song can present a challenge when the existing material has rhythmic and melodic or harmonic content. You have to make sure that the recycled recording plays at the current project's key signature and tempo.

Beginning with Logic 10.4, Smart Tempo allows you to automatically match the tempo of an imported audio file to the project tempo, while the Transpose parameter in the Region inspector makes it a breeze to change the pitch of that imported file.

1   Choose File > Project Settings > Smart Tempo.

2   Click the 'Set imported audio files to' pop-up menu, and choose On. Close the Settings
    window.

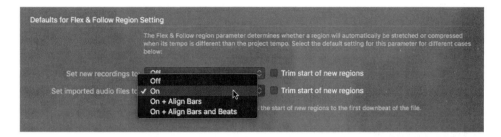

Logic will analyze any audio file you import to detect its original tempo, and time-stretch
it, as necessary, to make it play back at the project tempo. Let's import a guitar part.

3   In the control bar, click the Browsers button, and in the Browser pane, click the
    All Files tab.

4   Navigate to Logic Pro X Files > Media > Additional Media.

    Before importing **Groovy Guitar.wav**, let's try to play it along with the project.

5   In the control bar, click the Play button to play the project.

6   In the All Files Browser, select **Groovy Guitar.wav**, and click the Preview button, or
    press Option-Spacebar.

    It's pretty obvious that the guitar wasn't recorded at the same tempo as the current
    project.

7   Drag **Groovy Guitar** below the cymbal track at bar 1.

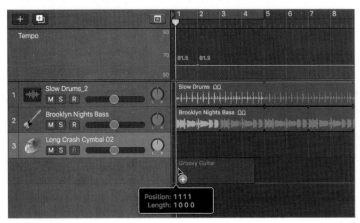

A progress bar appears while Logic analyzes the file, and then an alert asks if you want to show the File Tempo Editor, which allows you to perform more advanced tasks, such as editing the beats detected by Logic in the imported audio file. You won't need to perform such tasks for this exercise.

8   Click Don't Show to dismiss the alert.

9   Play the project from the beginning.

The guitar plays in the wrong key! You will fix that later, but for now, let's focus on the timing of the guitar.

10   In the bass track header (track 2), click the Mute (M) button to mute the track.

11   Listen to the project.

The guitar and the drums play in time. Let's now make the guitar play in the right key. The guitar was recorded in D minor, while the current project's key signature is E minor, so you need to transpose the guitar two semitones up.

12 Makes sure the *Groovy Guitar* region is selected, and in the Region inspector, double-click to the right of the Transpose parameter.

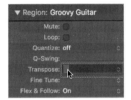

13 Enter *2*, and press Return.

The amount of transposition is indicated to the right of the region name (+2).

14 Unmute the bass track (track 2).

15 Listen to the project.

The guitar now plays at both the correct tempo and key signature. It still ends too early, and in the following exercise you will take care of copying the guitar a few times to make sure it fills up the guitar track.

Adding a Turntable or Tape Slow-Down Effect

When you stop a turntable with the stylus on the record, or stop a tape machine while keeping the playhead in contact with the magnetic tape, the result is a sound that drops in pitch as it slows down. This highly recognizable effect has recently regained popularity along with its opposite—the sound rising in pitch as speed increases when the tape transport or turntable starts.

You will now make copies of the guitar region and apply the turntable stop effect to the end of the guitar track.

1   Option-drag the *Groovy Guitar* region to bar 5, and then Option-drag it again to bar 9.

To add the turntable stop effect to the end of the last guitar region, you first need to create a volume fade.

2   Control-Shift-drag over the last *Groovy Guitar* region's end to create a fade-out starting at bar 13.

Let's turn that volume fade into a speed fade.

3   Control-click the fade-out and choose Slow Down.

The fade-out turns orange, indicating that it is now a speed fade.

4   Listen to your fade. It sounds just like a turntable stopping!

You can adjust the length and curve of the speed fade just as you would a volume fade. As you listen, adjust the fade's curve and length as follows:

5   Control-Shift-drag the middle of the fade to adjust its curve.

6   Control-Shift-drag the left edge of the fade to adjust its length.

7   Choose File > Close Project without saving the project.

You just used a speed fade to create a realistic turntable stop effect, but you can use speed fades for many kinds of effects. Try applying multiple rapid speed fades to short regions to create DJ scratching effects. Or add a speed fade at the end of a kick sample to make it drop in pitch.

Creating Tempo Changes and Tempo Curves

When you want to vary the tempo throughout a project, you can use the Tempo track to insert tempo changes and tempo curves. All MIDI regions and Apple Loops automatically follow the project tempo, even when tempo variations occur in the middle of a region. The **Groovy Guitar** is not an Apple Loop, but earlier you chose to automatically turn on Flex and Follow Tempo for imported audio files, so that region will also follow the proj- ect's tempo curve.

Creating and Naming Tempo Sets

In this exercise, you will create a new tempo set, and name both the current and new tempo sets. You will create a new tempo curve in the new tempo set, and later switch between the original tempo and the new tempo curve.

1   In the Tempo track header, from the Tempo pop-up menu, choose Tempo Sets > Rename Set.

A text field appears on the Tempo track header.

2 Enter *Original*, and press Return.

3 From the Tempo pop-up menu, choose Tempo Sets > New Set.

A new tempo set is created with a default value of 120 bpm. A text entry field appears, ready for you to enter a name for the new set. In this set, you will make the tempo go gradually faster, so let's name it Accelerando.

4 Rename the new tempo set *Accelerando*, and listen to the song.

All tracks in the project play at the new tempo (120 bpm).

Creating Tempo Changes and Tempo Curves

You now have two tempo sets, and you will edit the new one to create a tempo that starts at a 62 bpm tempo and progressively ramps up to about 90 bpm within the first couple of bars.

1 In the Tempo track, drag the tempo line down to 60 bpm.

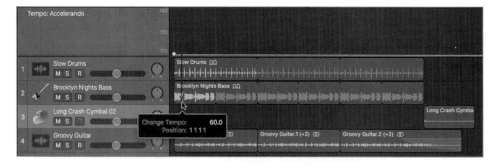

Although the line seems to stop at the bottom edge of the Tempo track, keep dragging down until you see the desired tempo value displayed in the help tag. When you release the mouse button, the scale in the Tempo track header updates and you can see the new tempo.

Let's insert a tempo change at bar 3.

2   Click the tempo line at bar 3.

A new tempo point is inserted at bar 3 with the current 60 bpm value.

3   Drag the line that is located to the right of the new tempo change up to a value of 90 bpm. Listen to the tempo change.

NOTE ▸ To reposition a tempo point, drag the tempo point horizontally.

4   Listen to the song.

The tempo changes abruptly at bar 3. To smooth the tempo change, you're going to accelerate the tempo from 60 bpm at bar 1 to 90 bpm at bar 3.

5   At bar 3, position the mouse pointer on the corner below the 90 bpm tempo point.

6   Drag the tempo point upward and to the left.

You can precisely adjust the tempo curve by dragging the tempo point farther to the left, up, or in both directions.

7   Listen to the song.

The tempo now ramps up progressively between bar 1 and bar 3.

8   Click the Global Tracks button (or press G) to close the global tracks.

9   Choose File > Close Project, but do not save the project.

You can create complex tempo maps to add excitement to your arrangements. Sometimes, a chorus that's a bit faster than the rest of the song is all an arrangement needs to really take off. Or you can use tempo curves to create the classic ritardando at the end of a song. All your Apple Loops and MIDI regions will automatically follow the tempo map, and you can use a flex mode for each audio track you want to follow the tempo map.

Making One Track Follow the Groove of Another Track

Playing all tracks at the same tempo is not always sufficient to achieve a tight rhythm. You also need to make sure they play with the same groove. For example, a musician may play slightly late to create a laid-back feel, or he may add some swing to his performance by delaying only the upbeats. On another track, notes may be placed on a rigid grid.

To learn how to get your tracks in the same groove, you will open a new project with a drummer playing a swing groove, and then make a shaker on another track follow the groove of the drummer.

1   Open Logic Pro X Files > Lessons > **07 Swing Groove**, and listen to the song.

Even though both tracks play at the same tempo, they are not synchronized. The drums (track 1) are playing a hip-hop shuffle groove while the shaker is playing on a straight sixteenth-note grid. Feel free to solo the individual tracks to clearly hear each instrument's feel.

Let's zoom in so you can see the individual drum hits on the waveforms.

2   Press Return to go back to the beginning of the project.

3   Press Command-Right Arrow nine times to zoom in on the first two beats (so you can clearly see 1 and 1.2 in the ruler).

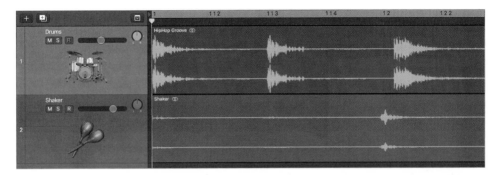

Below the 1.2 grid mark in the ruler, you can clearly see that the waveforms on the two tracks are out of sync.

To make the shaker follow the groove of the drums, you need to set the Drums track as the groove track.

4   Control-click a track header, and from the shortcut menu, choose Track Header Component > Groove Track.

At first glance, nothing seems to have changed in the track headers.

5   Position the mouse pointer over the track number (1) of the Drums track.

A gold star appears in place of the track number.

6   Click the gold star.

The gold star appears in a new column on the track header to indicate that the Drums track is now the groove track. On the Shaker track header, in the same column, you can select the checkbox to make that track follow the groove track.

7   On the Shaker track, select the Match Groove Track checkbox.

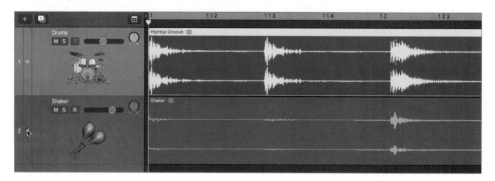

The waveform on the Shaker track updates so that the notes are in sync with the notes on the groove track.

8   Listen to the song. The shaker now follows the groove of the drums, and they play in sync.

9   Solo the Shaker track.

10   While listening to the shaker, deselect and select the Match Groove Track checkbox to compare the original performance with the new groove.

When the checkbox is deselected, the shaker plays straight eighth notes and sixteenth notes.

When the checkbox is selected, the shaker plays the same hip-hop shuffle feel as the drums.

11   Unsolo the Shaker track.

12   Choose File > Close Project without saving the project.

Groove tracks work with all track types (audio, software instrument, and Drummer tracks). Experiment by applying the groove of a sample to your MIDI programming or by making a Drummer track follow the groove of a live bass recording.

Change the Playback Pitch and Speed with Varispeed

In the days of analog tape recording, engineers performed all sorts of tricks by changing the tape speed. Many major albums were sped up ever so slightly during the mixing process to add excitement to tracks by raising their tempos. This simultaneously raised the pitch, giving the impression of the vocalist reaching higher notes in the most emotional passages of the song. On the other hand, engineers would sometimes slow the tape during recording so that a musician could play a challenging passage at a more comfortable tempo. When played back at its regular speed during mixdown, the recording created the illusion of the musician playing faster. DJs are probably the biggest users of Varispeed techniques, which gives them control over the tempo and pitch of a track, allowing for seamless transitions from one track to the next.

Logic takes this concept a step further, offering both the classic Varispeed—which, like a tape or record player, changes both the pitch and the speed—and a Speed Only mode, which allows you to change the speed without changing the pitch.

1   Open Logic Pro X Files > Lessons > **07 Little Lady**, and listen to the song. In the LCD display in the control bar, you can see that the song is in the key of A minor and its tempo is 152 bpm.

To use the Varispeed feature, you must add the Varispeed display to the control bar.

2   Control-click an empty space in the control bar, and from the shortcut menu, choose "Customize Control Bar and Display."

In the dialog's LCD column, the Varispeed option is dimmed. To turn it on, you first need to choose the custom LCD display.

3   In the LCD column, from the pop-up menu, choose Custom.

4   Below the pop-up menu, select Varispeed, and click OK.

A new Varispeed display appears in the custom LCD display.

5   In the Varispeed display, drag the 0.00% value up to 6.00%.

The Varispeed display is shaded in orange. The tempo value turns orange, too, indicating that the song is no longer playing at its normal tempo due to the Varispeed feature. If your main window is wide enough to display all the buttons to the right of the LCD display, you'll see the Varispeed button turn orange to indicate that the feature is enabled.

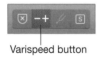

Varispeed button

6   Listen to the song.

The song plays faster but retains its original pitch. Let's check the song's current tempo.

7   In the Varispeed display, click the % symbol, and from the pop-up menu, choose Resulting Tempo.

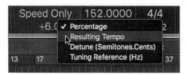

The Varispeed display shows the resulting tempo of 161.120 bpm. You can now use the display to set the desired playback tempo.

8   Double-click the 161.120 tempo value, and enter *140* bpm.

The song plays slower but still at its original pitch. This would be perfect for practicing a part by playing along with your instrument. You could even record your part at this speed, and then turn off Varispeed to play the whole song (including your newly recorded part) at the normal speed.

Now let's apply the classic Varispeed effect that changes both the playback speed and pitch.

9   In the Varispeed display, click Speed Only, and from the pop-up menu, choose Varispeed (Speed and Pitch).

10 Listen to the song.

Now the song plays both slower and lower in pitch. This is the classic Varispeed effect available on tape machines and turntables.

11 In the Varispeed display, click the bpm symbol, and from the pop-up menu, choose Detune (Semitones.Cents).

12 Double-click the −1.42 detune value, and enter *−1.00*.

13 Listen to the song.

Now the song plays slower and pitched down by one semitones. If your singer isn't at the top of her game that day and can't reach her usual high notes, you could record at this slower speed and later turn off Varispeed to play the whole song at the higher pitch.

14 In the control bar, click the Varispeed button to turn it off.

Editing the Timing of an Audio Region

You were introduced to Flex Time editing in Lesson 3 when you used it to tighten the rhythm of a few dead notes on a guitar. You will now go further and explore other Flex Time editing techniques while examining what happens to an audio waveform "under the hood."

Time-Stretching the Waveform Between Transient Markers

In this exercise, you will dive deeper into Flex Time editing by using it to correct the timing of a guitar.

1   From the global Marker track, drag the Breakdown marker (at bar 75) into the upper half of the ruler.

A cycle area is created that corresponds to the Breakdown marker.

2   Solo the two Gtr Bridge tracks (tracks 13 and 14).

3   Listen to the first three bars of the Breakdown section.

The two guitars on the soloed tracks play the same rhythm, but in two places the guitars are not hitting the notes together (bar 75, beat 2; and bar 77, beat 2).

4   In the Tracks area menu bar, click the Show/Hide Flex button (or press Command-F).

Show/Hide Flex button

The Tracks area is zoomed in vertically, and each track header shows a Track Flex button and a Flex pop-up menu.

5   Scroll and zoom in to the workspace so you can see the beginning of the *Gtr Bridge L* region (at bar 75) at the upper left of the workspace, right below the ruler.

6   Click the lower half of the ruler at bar 75 to position the playhead. Click track 13 to select it, and drag the zoom sliders (or press the Command-Arrow keys) to continue adjusting your zoom level so that you can see the first three beats of bar 75 in the ruler (the 75, 75.2, and 75.3 grid marks).

Remember that zooming with the zoom sliders or the Command-Arrow keys keeps the playhead at the same horizontal position in the workspace, and the selected track at the same vertical position in the Tracks area. Here, the beginning of the *Gtr Bridge L* region stays anchored at the upper left of the workspace.

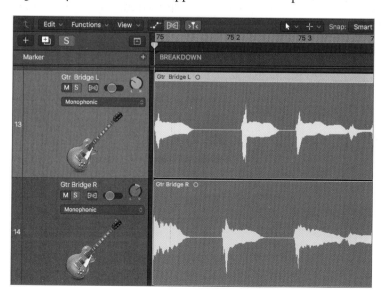

7   In the Gtr Bridge L track header (track 13), click the Track Flex button.

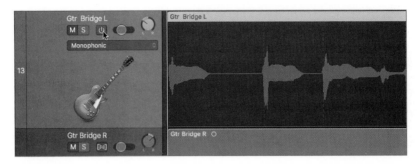

Flex editing is turned on. The region on the track is darker, and transient markers appear where Logic detected the attack of a new note. Logic automatically detects the most appropriate Flex Time mode for the track, which is set to Monophonic.

NOTE ▸ Monophonic mode is intended for instruments that produce only one pitch at a time (vocals, wind). Polyphonic is used with instruments that play chords (piano, guitar), and Slicing is for moving notes without time-stretching any audio (good for drums).

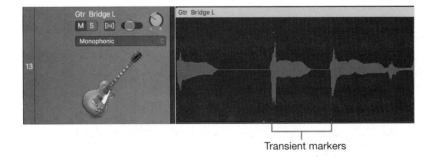

Transient markers

On track 13, the second note in the region is late. It should be in time with the second note of the *Gtr Bridge R* region on track 14 (under the 75.2 grid mark in the ruler).

8   In the upper half of the waveform, place the mouse pointer over the transient marker of the second note.

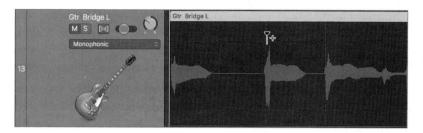

The mouse pointer turns into a Flex tool and looks like a single flex marker with a + (plus sign) next to it. This symbol indicates that clicking or dragging will insert one flex marker on the transient marker. When you drag the flex marker, the waveform is stretched between the region beginning and the flex marker, and between the flex marker and the region end. Let's try it.

9   Drag the Flex tool to the left to align the flex marker with the second note of the track below.

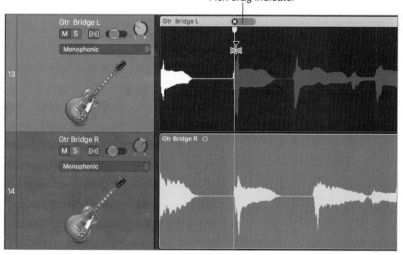

Flex drag indicator

When the mouse pointer is positioned over a flex marker, a flex drag indicator in the region header above the flex marker shows how the flex marker was moved from its original position. You can click the X symbol inside the flex drag indicator to delete that flex marker (and return the waveform to its original state).

After you release the mouse button, the flex marker looks like a bright vertical line with a handle at the top.

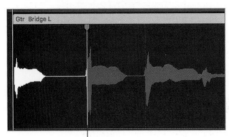

Flex marker

The waveform to the left of the flex marker is white, indicating that it was time compressed. The waveform to the right of the flex marker was time expanded. As a result, all the notes to the right of the flex marker have changed their positions, which is not what's wanted here.

10 Choose Edit > Undo (or press Command-Z).

11 In the lower half of the waveform, place the mouse pointer over the transient marker of the second note.

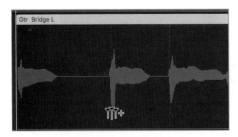

The Flex tool looks like three flex markers with a + (plus sign). Clicking it creates three flex markers, one at each of the following positions:

▶ On the transient marker you're about to drag

▶ On the transient marker before (which will not move)

▶ On the transient marker after (which will not move)

12 Drag the Flex tool to the left to align the note with the second note of the track below.

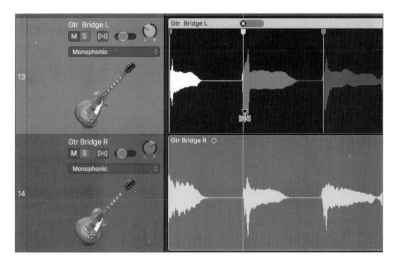

The first note is time compressed, the second note is time expanded, and the rest of the region remains unaffected.

13 Listen to the edit.

The timing sounds much better than in the original. However, the first note is now slightly shorter and the second note longer. It's a subtle difference, but in the next exercise you will use another technique to get a tighter result.

14 Choose Undo > Dragging (or press Command-Z) to undo the change.

Moving Waveform Sections Without Time-Stretching

In the previous exercise, you applied the Flex tool to time-stretch a waveform using either the previous and next transient markers or the region's beginning and end points as boundaries.

Now you will create a flex marker after the first note so that no time-stretching occurs before that marker. You will then use the Marquee, your current Command-click tool, to select a section of the waveform, and move it without time-stretching the selection.

1 In the *Gtr Bridge L* region, place your mouse pointer in the upper half of the waveform, away from transient markers.

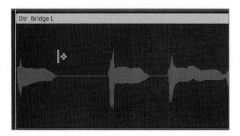

The cursor looks like a single flex marker with a + (plus sign).

2 Click the upper half of the waveform, after the end of the first note, to create a flex marker.

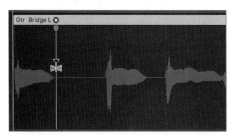

TRACTION AVE.
→ 700 E.

DISTANT
COUSINS

WWW.DISTANTCOUSINSOFFICIAL.COM

    MUSIC